Published by Design Community College Inc.

Design Community College Inc.
PO Box 1153
Topanga CA 90290 USA

info@curedale.com
Designed and illustrated by Robert Curedale

ISBN-10: 1-940805-15-5
ISBN-13: 978-1-940805-15-3

DESIGN THINKING
POCKET GUIDE: 2ND EDITION

Robert Curedale

PUBLISHED BY DESIGN COMMUNITY COLLEGE LOS ANGELES

"

Design Thinking is all about creating intelligent change

INTRODUCTION

Over the last decade design has moved from being a tool of marketing towards being an imperative for intelligent change. It has become less about making people want things through advertising and marketing and more about making things people want through good design that answers human need. This is Design Thinking and it is a better way of thinking. It is less about ego, fame and desire and more about collaboration and human need.

In 2008 I established a number of social networks for working designers. These groups have grown to over one million members and may now constitute the largest global network of working designers. I have been spreading the word about the value of Design Thinking through this huge network, presenting on-line classes and publishing books about Design Thinking. This book incorporates the evolution of ideas that has happened in the field over the years since I published the first book "Design Thinking Process and Methods Manual"

There has been a rapidly growing interest in Design Thinking. Recently large corporations including Pepsi and IBM announced major initiatives to train their staff and adopt Design Thinking. Design Thinking is an approach to designing products, services, architecture, spaces and experiences as well as complex systems of these things that is being quickly adopted by designers. The list of world's leading brands that are using it has grown considerably from the introduction in my first book and now includes such as GE, Pepsico, Target, Deloitte Innovation, SAP, Singapore And Australian Governments, Procter And Gamble, Whirlpool, Bayer, BMW, DHL, Daimler, Deutsche Bank, Philips Electronics, Infosys, AirBnB, Autodesk, Bank Of America, Mayo Clinic, Steelcase, Black & Decker, Mattel, Microsoft, Miele, Airbus, Panasonic, Shell Innovation Research, Glaxosmithkline, Nike, Cisco, Jetblue, Kaiser Permanent, Unilever, Electrolux Arup, IDEO and Intuit. It is being taught at leading universities including Stanford, Yale and Harvard.

Design Thinking creates practical and innovative solutions to problems. It drives repeatable innovation and business value. Design Thinking can be used to develop a wide range of products, services, experiences as well as design and business strategy. It is an approach that can be applied by anyone. Design Thinking can also be fun. I hope that you will find this third book useful.

CONTENTS

Introduction

Contents

Chapter 9
Implement & Deliver

"

Design Thinking is about changing from:

Making people want things [through advertising and marketing] to making things people want

PIETER BAERT
Service consultant

DESIGN THINKING HABITS

"

Design Thinkers
create for others first

"

Good design

Is innovative
Makes a product useful
Is aesthetic
Makes a product understandable
Is unobtrusive
Is honest
Is long-lasting
Is thorough down to the last detail
Is environmentally friendly
Is as little design as possible

DIETER RAMS
Industrial Designer.

UNMET USER NEED

- ●
- ●
- ●
- ●

define the
problem

test learn
refine

understand the
user identify
unmet needs

DESIGN THINKING
PROCESS

prototype

create ideas

- ●
- ●
- ●
- ●

DESIGN SOLUTION

DESIGN THINKING

WHAT IS DESIGN THINKING?

Design Thinking is or approach to designing that supports innovation and intelligent change. Design Thinking is a human-centered approach which is driven by creative and analytical thinking, customer empathy and iterative learning.

It involves a toolkit of methods that can be applied to different problems by cross disciplinary groups or by individuals. Anyone can use Design Thinking. It can be fun.

WHO INVENTED IT?

The origins of Design Thinking date back to before the 1950s. Design Thinking adopted ideas that came from the creativity methods of the 1950s, the design science and design methods movements of the 1960s, user centered design movement of the 1980s and experience and service design from the 2,000s. In 1987 Peter Rowe, a Professor at the Harvard Graduate School of Design, published "Design Thinking" the first significant usage of the term "Design Thinking" in literature. After 2000 the term became widely used.

WHY USE DESIGN THINKING?

Design Thinking is useful when you have:
1. A poorly defined problem.
2. A lack of information.
3. A changing context or environment
4. It should result in consistently innovative solutions.

Design Thinking seeks a balance of design considerations including:
1. Business.
2. Appropriate application of technology
3. Empathy with people.
4. Environmental consideration.

Design Thinking seeks to balance two modes of thinking:
1. Analytical thinking
2. Creative Thinking

WHAT CAN IT BE APPLIED TO?
1. Products
2. Services
3. Experiences
4. Interactions
5. Systems of the above

DESIGN THINKING PROCESS

Design Thinking has a particular process

1. Define intent
2. Through ethnographic research develop empathy for the point of view of the user.
3. Synthesize the research
4. Frame insights
5. Explore Concepts
6. Synthesize the concepts generated
7. Prototype the favored ideas
8. Test the prototypes with users
9. Incorporate changes
10. Iterate prototype and testing till a workable design is reached
11. Implement
12. Deliver Offering

RESOURCES

Multidisciplinary team of 4 to 12 people
A project space
Post it notes
Dry erase markers
White board
Digital camera
Copy paper
Chairs
Large table

WHO CAN USE DESIGN THINKING?

Design Thinking is a technique for everyone and any problem. Design Thinking process involves many stakeholders in working together to find a balanced design solution. The designer is a member of a type of design orchestra. The customer is involved throughout the design process and works with the design team to communicate their needs and desires and to help generate design solutions that are relevant to them.

The many methods used help anyone to understand the diverse perspectives of the many stakeholders. It takes some courage to listen and recognize the point of view of the stakeholders. Managers, designers, social scientists, engineers marketers, stakeholders customers and others can collaborate creatively to apply Design Thinking to everyone's benefit.

The process is one of co-creation and the designer is a listener and a facilitator. Everyone adds value to the design. Design Thinking is not just for professional designers. Everyone can contribute. Many schools are now teaching Design Thinking to children as an approach that can be applied to life.

20 WAYS DESIGN THINKING IS BEING USED

1. Service provision, which is sold to customers for better solution finding or as a program for internal change

2. New product and service development/improvement

3. Better alignment, collaboration and knowledge transfer

4. Empathy for the customer: gaining a better understanding of the customer and user

5. Improving own internal business processes and organizational structures

6. Commercial innovation and more efficient insight-driven marketing campaigns

7. Internal staff training for human/customer-centered mindset.

8. Toolbox. Adapting specific tools and methods to fit an individual purpose

9. Development of better teaching and training formats

10. Increasing creativity in teams

11. Customer engagement and co-creation

12. Public relations and reputation management vehicle

13. Service and experience design improvement

14. Test assumptions and iterate solutions

15. New business models and go-to-market strategies

16. Attractive recruiting tool

17. Means for more efficient meetings and arrangements

18. Generating demand and better customer acquisition via workshops

19. Improving the innovation process

20. Means for improving the style of design outcomes

2015 study by Hasso-Plattner-Institut für softwaresystemtechnik an der Universität Potsdam, September 2015 of 235 German and international companies of all sizes

CHARACTERISTICS OF DESIGN THINKERS

D.SCHOOL BOOT CAMP BOOTLEG (2009)	D.SCHOOL BOOT CAMP BOOTLEG (2010)	TIM BROWN (2008)	BAECK & GREMETT (2011)	COMMENT
Focus on human values	Focus on human values	Empathy	Empathy	"Focus on human values" includes empathy for users and feedback from them.
Create clarity from complexity	Craft clarity	Integrative thinking	Ambiguity Curiosity Holistic Open mindset	All these items refer to styles of thinking. "Clarity" refers to producing a coherent vision out of messy problems. Baeck & Gremett focus on attitudes of the Design Thinker.
		Optimism		Only mentioned by Tim Brown, but seems to be regarded as a universal characteristic of Design Thinkers.
Get experimental and experiential	Embrace experimentation	Experimentalism	Curiosity Open mindset	Experimentation is an integral part of the designer's work.
Collaborate across boundaries	Radical collaboration	Collaboration	Collaborative	Refers to the collaboration between people from different disciplines (having different backgrounds and viewpoints).
Show, do not tell Bias toward action	Show, do not tell Bias toward action			Emphasizes action, for example, by creating meaningful prototypes and confronting potential users with them.
Be mindful of process	Be mindful of process			Emphasizes that Design Thinkers need to keep the overall process (which is regarded as a core element of Design Thinking, in mind with respect to methods and goals.

Source: Gerd Waloszek, SAP AG, SAP User Experience – September 1, 2013

EVOLUTION OF DESIGN THINKING

YEAR	DESIGN MOVEMENT	DESIGN APPROACHES	PEOPLE
2010s	Design Thinking	Experience design	David Kelley
		Creative class	Tim Brown
			Roger Martin
			Rolf Faste
2000s	Service Design	Human Centered Design	Lucy Kimbell
1990s	Process Methods	Meta Design	Ezio Manzini
			William Rause
			Richard Buchanan
1980s	Cognitive Reflections	User Centered Design	Don Norman
			Donal Schon
			Nigel Cross
			Peter Rowe
			Bryan Lawson
1970s			Robert McKim
1960s	Design Science	Participatory Design	Horst Rittel
		Design Methods	Herbet Simon
			Bruce Archer
1950s	Creativity Methods	Brainstorming	Alex Osborn

ATTRIBUTES OF DESIGN THINKING

AMBIGUITY	Being comfortable when things are unclear or when you do not know the answer	Design Thinking addresses wicked ill-defined and tricky problems.
COLLABORATIVE	Working together across disciplines	People design in interdisciplinary teams.
CONSTRUCTIVE	Creating new ideas based on old ideas, which can also be the most successful ideas	Design Thinking is a solution-based approach that looks for an improved future result.
CURIOSITY	Being interested in things you do not understand or perceiving things with fresh eyes	Considerable time and effort is spent on clarifying the requirements. A large part of the problem solving activity, then, consists of problem definition and problem shaping.
EMPATHY	Seeing and understanding things from your customers' point of view	The focus is on user needs (problem context).
HOLISTIC	Looking at the bigger context for the customer	Design Thinking attempts to meet user needs and also drive business success.
ITERATIVE	A cyclical process where improvements are made to a solution or idea regardless of the phase	The Design Thinking process is typically non-sequential and may include feedback loops and cycles (see below).
NON JUDGMENTAL	Creating ideas with no judgment toward the idea creator or the idea	Particularly in the brainstorming phase, there are no early judgments.
OPEN MINDSET	Embracing Design Thinking as an approach for any problem regardless of industry or scope	The method encourages "outside the box thinking" ("wild ideas"); it defies the obvious and embraces a more experimental approach.

Core Attributes of Design Thinking from Baeck & Gremett, 2011

THE TEN FACES OF INNOVATION

ANTHROPOLOGIST	Excels at human observation and research
EXPERIMENTER	Tests ideas through trial and error
CROSS-POLLINATOR	Finds ideas from other industries and cultures
HURDLER	Finds a way around obstacles
COLLABORATOR	Brings groups together
DIRECTOR	Helps select and guide the team
EXPERIENCE ARCHITECT	Considers the experience of the user
SET DESIGNER	Creates an environment for teams to work
CAREGIVER	Knows the customer's needs before they do
STORYTELLER	Communicates within and outside the company

The ten faces of Innovation: David Kelley

DESIGN THINKING PROCESS

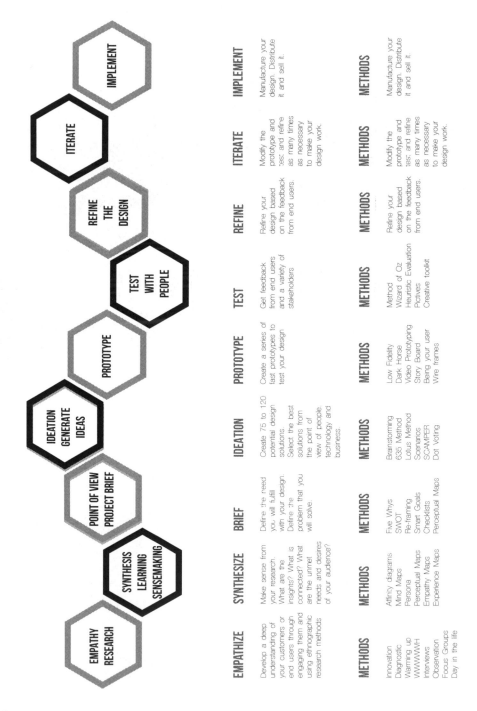

EMPATHIZE	SYNTHESIZE	BRIEF	IDEATION	PROTOTYPE	TEST	REFINE	ITERATE	IMPLEMENT
Develop a deep understanding of your customers or end users through engaging them and using ethnographic research methods	Make sense from your research. What are the insights? What is connected? What are the unmet needs and desires of your audience?	Define the need you will fulfill with your design. Define the problem that you will solve	Create 75 to 120 potential design solutions. Select the best solutions from the point of view of people, technology and business.	Create a series of fast prototypes to test your design	Get feedback from end users and a variety of stakeholders	Refine your design based on the feedback from end users.	Modify the prototype and test and refine as many times as necessary to make your design work.	Manufacture your design. Distribute it and sell it.
METHODS	**METHODS**	**METHODS**	**METHODS**	**METHODS**	**METHODS**	**METHODS**	**METHODS**	**METHODS**
Innovation Diagnostic Warming up WWWWWH Interviews Observation Focus Groups Day in the life	Affinity diagrams Mind Maps Persona Perceptual Maps Empathy Maps Experience Maps	Five Whys SWOT Re-framing Smart Goals Checklists Perceptual Maps	Brainstorming 635 Method Lotus Method Scenarios SCAMPER Dot Voting	Low Fidelity Dark Horse Video Prototyping Story Board Being your user Wire frames	Method Wizard of Oz Heuristic Evaluation Pictives Creative toolkit	Refine your design based on the feedback from end users.	Modify the prototype and test and refine as many times as necessary to make your design work.	Manufacture your design. Distribute it and sell it.

DESIGN THINKING PROCESS

GOALS?
What are we looking for?

1. Meet with key stakeholders to set vision
2. Assemble a diverse team
3. Develop intent and vision
4. Explore scenarios of user experience
5. Document user performance requirements
6. Define the group of people you are designing for. What is their gender, age, and income range. Where do they live. What is their culture?
7. Define your scope and constraints
8. Identify a need that you are addressing. Identify a problem that you are solving.
9. Identify opportunities
10. Meet stakeholders

DISCOVER EMPATHIZE RESEARCH
What else is out there?

1. Identify what you know and what you need to know.
2. Document a research plan
3. Benchmark competitive products
4. Create a budgeting and plan.
5. Create tasks and deliverables
6. Explore the context of use
7. Understand the risks
8. Observe and interview individuals, groups, experts.
9. Develop design strategy
10. Undertake qualitative, quantitative, primary and secondary research.
11. Talk to vendors

SYNTHESIZE
What have we learned?

1. Review the research.
2. Make sense out of the research
3. Develop insights
4. Cluster insights
5. Create a hierarchy

DEVELOP A UNIQUE POINT OF VIEW
What is the design brief?

IDEATE
How is this for starters?

1. Brainstorm
2. Define the most promising ideas
3. Refine the ideas
4. Establish key differentiation of your ideas
5. Investigate existing intellectual property.

PROTOTYPE TEST AND ITERATE
How could we make it better?

1. Make your favored ideas physical.
2. Create low-fidelity prototypes from inexpensive available materials
3. Develop question guides
4. Develop test plan
5. Test prototypes with stakeholders
6. Get feedback from people.
7. Refine the prototypes
8. Test again
9. Build in the feedback
10. Refine again.
11. Continue iteration until design works.
12. Document the process.

13. When you are confident that your idea works make a prototype that looks and works like a production product.

IMPLEMENT AND DELIVER
Let's make it. Let's sell it.

1. Create your proposed production design
2. Test and evaluate
3. Review objectives
4. Manufacture your first samples
5. Review first production samples and refine.
6. Launch
7. Obtain user feedback
8. Conduct field studies
9. Define the vision for the next product or service.

DESIGN THINKING PROCESS MODELS

HAYES 1989	AMABILE 1989	PLATTNER 2009 DESIGN THINKING	KOLKO 2007	IDEO KELLEY 2002	TREFFINGER 1992	ROOZENBURG 1995
	task presentation	understand		understand	mess finding	function
identify the problem	preparation	observe	research	observe	data finding	analysis
problem representation		point of view	synthesis			synthesis
planning the solution	idea generation	ideate			problem finding	
execute the plan		prototype	ideation		idea finding	
evaluate the plan	idea validation	test	refinement	visualize		simulation
				evaluate and refine	solution finding	evaluation

Phase	WIKIPEDIA HERBERT SIMON	IDEO TOOLKIT	TIMBROWN IDEO	D.SCHOOL D-SCHOOL HP	D.SCHOOL BOOTCAMP BOOTLEG HPIMODES	BAECK & GREMETT 2011	MARK DZIERSK FAST COMPANY
Understand the problem	define	discovery	inspiration	understand	empathize: observe, engage, immerse	define the problem to solve	define the problem
observe users	research			observe		look for inspiration	
interpret the results		interpretation		point of view	define problem statement		
generate ideas	ideation	ideation	ideation	ideate	ideate	ideate	create many options
prototype experiment	**prototype**	experimentation	implement	prototype	prototype	generate prototypes	refine directions repeat
test, implement, improve	objectives/ choose implement learn	evolution		evolution	test refine and improve solutions	solicit user feedback	pick the winner, execute

Source: this page adapted from Gerd Waloszek, SAP AG, SAP User Experience 2012

Why Design Thinking should be at the core of your design and business strategies

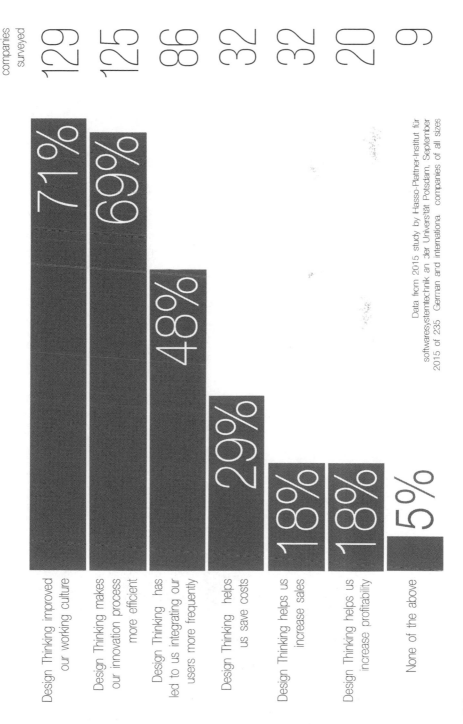

Number of companies surveyed

	Number of companies surveyed	Percentage
Design Thinking improved our working culture	129	71%
Design Thinking makes our innovation process more efficient	125	69%
Design Thinking has led to us integrating our users more frequently	86	48%
Design Thinking helps us save costs	32	29%
Design Thinking helps us increase sales	32	18%
Design Thinking helps us increase profitability	20	18%
None of the above	9	5%

Data from 2015 study by Hasso-Plattner-Institut für softwaresystemtechnik an der Universität Potsdam, September 2015 of 235 German and international companies of all sizes

Design Thinking is quickly gathering traction in industry. Chart of organizations years of Design Thinking experience [2015]

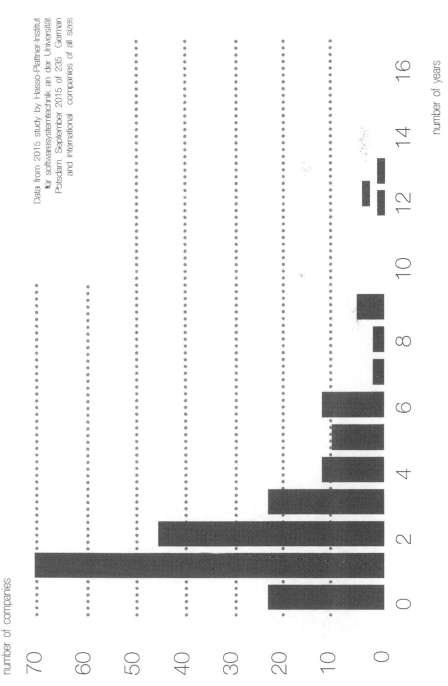

Data from 2015 study by Hasso-Plattner-Institut für softwaresystemtechnik an der Universität Potsdam September 2015 of 235 German and international companies of all sizes

"

Design Thinking has a wide variety of tools that you can select to work on your design problem. There is usually more than one tool that can be used.

EMPATHY

Empathy is sometimes defined as 'standing in someone else's shoes' or 'seeing through someone else's eyes'. It is The ability to identify and understand another's situation, feelings and motives. In design it may be defined as: identifying with others and, adopting their perspective. Empathy is different to sympathy. Empathy does not necessarily imply compassion. Empathy is a respectful understanding of what others are experiencing and their point of view.

E.B. Titchener invented the word in 1909 in an attempt to translate the German word "Einfühlungsvermögen".

WHY HAVE EMPATHY
1. Empathy is a core skill for designers to design successfully for other people.
2. Empathy is needed for business success.
3. Empathy is needed for products and services to be adopted by the people we design for.
4. Empathy builds trust.

HOW TO PRACTICE EMPATHY

1. Put yourself in contact and the context of people who you are designing for.
2. Ask questions and listen to the answers.
3. Read between the lines
4. Observe.
5. Listen
6. Restating what you think you heard.
7. Recognize that people are individuals.
8. Notice body language. Most communication is non verbal
9. Withhold judgment when you hear views different to your own.
10. Take a personal interest in people

ITERATION
Design Thinking follows an iterative process. Iterative design is aimed at refining a design based on learning from user interaction. Iterative design is a cyclic process of prototyping, testing, and refining a product, system service, experience or process. Following testing the most recent iteration of a design with end users, changes and refinements are made. This process is intended to improve the quality and functionality of a design. In iterative design, interaction with the design is used as a form of research for informing and evolving a

SHOSHIN: THE BEGINNER'S MIND

WHAT IS IT

The phrase shoshin means beginner's mind. It refers to having an attitude of full of openness, enthusiasm, and fresh perspectives in learning something new, eagerness, and lack of preconceptions even at an advanced level, like a child.

Shoshin also means "correct truth" and is used to describe a genuine signature on a work of art. It is use to describe something that is perfectly genuine.

WHERE DID IT ORIGINATE?

1. Shoshin is a term from Zen Buddhism and Japanese martial arts.

HOW TO USE SHOSHIN

1. Withhold judgment. Do not suggest that an idea will not work or that it has negative side-effects. All ideas are potentially good so do not judge them until afterwards.
2. Observe and Listen
3. Ask why
4. Be curious
5. Look for new connections

WHY USE SHOSHIN

1. Sometimes expertise can create closed mindedness.
2. Our assumptions can stand in the way of creating new ideas. A beginner is not aware of biases that can stand in the way of a good new idea.
3. Our experience is an asset but our assumptions may be misconceptions and stereotypes,
4. Innovation often requires looking at a problem in a new way.
5. Beginner's minds can help make breakthroughs
6. Shoshin can transform a routine task into something more enjoyable and less stressful.
7. Observe and engage users without value judgments.
8. Question your assumptions. Ask why?
9. Be curious and explore.
10. Search for patterns and connections no one else has seen.
11. Be open and listen

"

Integrative thinking
is critical. You need
to balance business,
people issues,
aesthetics and usability,
application of the
best technologies
and consider the
environmental
consequences

"

Innovation is all about people. Innovation thrives when the population is diverse, accepting and willing to cooperate.

VIVEK WADHWA
Entrepreneur Researcher and Writer.

DIVERSITY

WHAT IS IT

Diversity means different genders, different ages, be from different cultures, different socioeconomic backgrounds and have different outlooks to be most successful.

WHY HAVE DIVERSITY

1. To attract good people
2. It broadens the customer base in a competitive environment.
3. Diversity brings substantial potential benefits such as better decision making and improved problem solving, greater creativity and innovation, which leads to enhanced product development, and more successful marketing to different types of customers. Diversity provides organizations with the ability to compete in global markets

HOW TO PROMOTE DIVERSITY

1. View employees as individuals.
2. Seek commitment from key participants.
3. Be open-minded. Recognize, and encourage employees to recognize, that one's own experience, background, and culture are not the only ones with value to the organization.
4. Articulate the benefits and motivations for becoming a more diverse organization.
5. Develop a definition of diversity that is linked to organizational mission.
6. Identify other organizations, both locally and nationally, that might serve
7. as models for diversity efforts.
8. Develop a realistic action plan for diversity efforts that takes into account ongoing operations and competing priorities.
9. Develop criteria to measure success. In other words, begin to build an evaluation plan.
10. Create a safe environment for candid and honest participation
11. Set relevant, pragmatic and achievable goals for bringing about organizational diversity.
12. Articulate expected outcomes and measures of change.

"

Design Thinking is
a good approach to
design for wicked
problems. These are
complex, risky, ill-
defined, changing, and
ambiguous problems

THINKING STYLES

ABDUCTIVE THINKING

With abductive reasoning, unlike deductive reasoning, the premises do not guarantee the conclusion. Abductive reasoning can be understood as "inference to the best explanation" Abductive reasoning typically begins with an incomplete set of observations and proceeds to the likeliest possible explanation for the set. It's goal is to explore what could possibly be true.

"A person or organization instilled with that discipline is constantly seeking a fruitful balance between reliability and validity, between art and science, between intuition and analytics, and between exploration and exploitation. The design-thinking organization applies the designer's most crucial tool to the problems of business. That tool is abductive reasoning." *Roger Martin*

Charles Sanders Peirce originated the term and argued that no new idea could come from inductive or deductive logic.

DEDUCTIVE THINKING

The process of reasoning from one or more general statements (premises) to reach a logically certain conclusion. Deductive reasoning is one of the two basic forms of valid reasoning. It begins with a general hypothesis or known fact and creates a specific conclusion from that generalization.

Described by Aristotle 384-322bce, Plato 428-347bce, and Pythagoras 582-500 BCE

INDUCTIVE THINKING

Inductive thinking is a kind of reasoning that constructs or evaluates general propositions that are derived from specific examples. Inductive reasoning contrasts with deductive reasoning, in which specific examples are derived from general propositions.

Described by Aristotle 384-322bce,

CRITICAL THINKING

"The process of actively and skillfully conceptualizing, applying, analyzing, synthesizing, and evaluating information to reach an answer or conclusion. disciplined thinking that is clear, rational, open-minded, and informed by evidence, willingness to integrate new or revised perspectives into our ways of thinking and acting"

Critical thinking is an important element of all professional fields and academic disciplines

DESIGN THINKING

Design Thinking is a formal method for practical, creative resolution of problems and creation of solutions, with the intent of an improved future result. In this regard it is a form of solution-based, or solution-focused thinking

Source: Wikipedia

BUSINESS THINKING	DESIGN THINKING	CREATIVE THINKING
Left Brain	Uses whole brain	Right brain
Rational	Both rational and intuitive	Emotional
Structured	Structured and intuitive	Intuitive
Analytical	Analytical and creative	Creative
Likes well defined problems	Works with defined and ill defined problems	Works with ill defined complex problems
Does not tolerate mistakes	Mistakes are inexpensive and a learning opportunity	Tolerates mistakes during exploration
Analyse then decide	Prototype test decide	Ideate then decide
Focuses on parts of a problem	Focuses on parts and on whole iteratively	Holistic diffuse focus
Convergent	Convergent and divergent	Divergent
Vertical	Vertical and Lateral	Lateral
Objective	Objective and subjective	Subjective
Linear	Linear and associative	Associative
Yes but	Yes and yes but	Yes and .....
Verbal and mathematical	Visual, verbal mathematical	Visual
The answer	Explores, tests iterates	One possible answer
Judges	Witholds judgent until tested	Withhold judgement
Probability	Possibility and probablity	Possibility
Improve	Improves and innovates	Innovate
Sequential	Sequential and synthesizing	Synthesizing
Analyze and evaluate	Imagines, synthesizes and tests	Imagine
Parts and details	Parts and the whole	Whole and big picture
Observe	Imagines and observes	Imagine
Facts	Story and facts	Story
Phases	Phases and dimesions	Dimensions
Sort and seperate	Sorts infuses and blends	Infuse and blend
Idependent	Indpendent and interdependednt	Interdependent
Successive	Successive and simultaneous	Simultaneous
Safe	takes risk but minimizes the cost of failure	Risk taking
Knows	Believes, tests and knows	Believes

CREATIVE & ANALYTICAL THINKING

CREATIVE THINKING
Right Brain
Traditional training of designers and artists

Explore
Generate ideas
Imagine possibilities
Re-frame
Build ideas
"Yes and what if?
Try different perspectives
Imagine extreme cases
Increase ideas

DIVERGENT THINKING

CONVERGENT THINKING

Make decisions
Clarify
Make sense
Decrease
Create hierarchies
Refine
Cluster
Connect
Test

ANALYTICAL THINKING
Left Brain
Traditional training of managers and engineers

Soiurce: Adapted from the center for Creati8ve Emergence

"

Our building which is Steve Jobs brainchild, is another way that we try to get people from different departments to interact. Most buildings are designed for some functional purpose, but ours is structured to maximize inadvertent encounters. At its center is a large atrium, which contains the cafeteria, meeting rooms, bathrooms and mailboxes. As a result everyone has strong reasons to go there repeatedly during the course of the workday. It's hard to describe just how valuable the resulting chance encounters are

ED CATMULL
President Pixar

DIVERGENT THINKING

Convergent thinking is a tool for problem solving in which the brain is applies a mechanized system or formula to some problem, where the solution is a number of steps from the problem. This kind of thinking is particularly appropriate in science6, engineering, maths and technology.

Convergent thinking is opposite from divergent thinking in which a person generates many unique, design solutions to a design problem. Divergent thinking is followed by convergent thinking, in which a designer assesses, judges, and strengthens those options. Divergent thinking is what we do when we do not know the answer, when we do not know

CONVERGENT THINKING

The design process is a series of divergent and convergent phases. During the divergent phase of design the designer creates a number of choices. The goal of this approach is to analyze alternative approaches to test for the most stable solution. Divergent thinking is what we do when we do not know the answer, when we do not know the next step. Divergent thinking is followed by convergent thinking, in which a designer assesses, judges, and strengthens those options.

DESIGN THINKING SPACES

1. Lightweight, comfortable, readily movable chairs perhaps on wheels can maximize a relatively small footprint and be arranged in multiple configurations
2. Show your work in progress and let people comment.
3. Surround yourself with the material that your team is working on.
4. Mobile large white boards 6 ft x 4 ft and pin boards.
5. Mobile boards can have a magnetic white board on one side and a pin board on the reverse side.
6. A laptop-sized surface for each attendee
7. Walls can be used for projection, writing, or pinning up information in areas visible to everyone
8. Acoustic privacy should be ensured.
9. Large walls can be used as display spaces.
10. Use work tools that are easily accessible
11. Think of every vertical surface as a potential space for displaying work
12. Use flexible technologies such as wi-fi that allow relocation of services such as internet and power connections.
13. Have a projector and screen
14. Team rooms should offer the flexibility to be arranged to suit the project at hand
15. Seating should allow all participants to see one another and read body language
16. Select furniture with wheels that can be easily moved
17. Small tables can be used for breakouts or grouped into a common surface
18. Ample writing and display areas, as well as surfaces for laying things out, support the need for visual cues and reference materials
19. Provide a large area of vertical displays such as walls white boards, pin boards, foam core boards, projection surfaces, that allow users to actively and flexibly interact with the information
20. Build spaces that support different types of collaboration.
21. Consider physical and virtual collaboration.
22. Spaces should be flexible for unplanned collaboration.
23. Position individual works paces around group spaces for flexibility
24. Provide comfortable group areas for informal interactions and information sharing.
25. The spaces need to be large enough to accommodate all the research materials,
26. visuals, and prototypes in order to keep them visible and accessible all of the time.

Source: Adapted from Haworth recommendations

CONTEXT

Context is external elements that influence a design. These elements are physical and non-physical. Roads, buildings, and land contour are examples for physical elements related to the context of architecture while non-physical elements are weather conditions, local culture, as well as political and economic constraints.

The environmental context relates to the time, the day, the location, the type of place and any other physical aspect that could influence your design.

The user context is about how people are different. It's about what every user likes, and dislikes It's also about the user's state of mind their habits and their state of mobility.

The surrounding context influences the success of a design

FRESH EYES

Outside people have a different perspective that may allow them to contribute new ideas and see problems with existing ideas and directions. Outsiders may have experiences from other industries that can help solve problems

Outside people may be aware of other people who can contribute something valuable. They may ask different questions. They may have relevant experiences that are lacking in your design team. At several points in your design process invite outsiders to review your design and give you feedback.

CROSS POLLINATION

Cross-pollination helps grow ideas. To solve complex problems, designers need to incorporate a wide range of styles, skills, and perspectives,

A team may lack diversity and not understand the perspective of end users.

The more we cross pollinate with other disciplines, the stronger our designs become.

Use cross disciplinary teams. Share ideas and observations with people outside your organization.

Travel can help your design team get exposed to new ways of looking at a problem.

Diversity including race, culture, gender, and income can help cross pollinate your design with different perspectives that may reflect your customer's perspectives.

Read outside your field. Talk to people in different industries

Design Thinking involves understanding your customers' needs, and building your products and services and experiencing life in their context.

BALANCED DESIGN

Design Thinking seeks to find an optimal balance between four factors.
1. Business needs, including return on investment, growth, price point, competitive advantage cash flow.
2. Technology. Selection of appropriate manufacturing methods and processes, materials and engineering approaches.
3. People's needs and desires. This includes the usability, and aesthetics.
4. Environmental factors. This includes environmental sustainability.

Designers have often in the past oriented designs towards people's needs and desires but been less successful balancing business, environmental and technological factors. Many businesses have oriented their goals towards business factors. Companies that find a sustainable balance between these factors develop a competitive advantage over companies that tend to be oriented towards one factor.

CROSS DISCIPLINARY COLLABORATION

Depending on the design challenge, design teams can engage anthropologists, engineers, educators, doctors, lawyers, scientists, etc. in the innovative problem solving process.

Design Thinking draws on the creative and analytical talents of the design team to reframe the design problem as needed. Design Thinking combines the wisdom and skills of many disciplines working in close and flexible collaboration. Each team member requires disciplinary empathy allowing them to work collaboratively with other discipline members.

COLLECTIVE INTELLIGENCE

Collective intelligence is a type of shared intelligence that emerges from the collaboration of many people and is expressed in consensus decision making

Collective intelligence requires four conditions to exist.
1. Openness Sharing ideas, experiences and perspectives
2. Peering People are free to share and build on each other's ideas freely.
3. Sharing knowledge, experiences ideas.
4. Acting Globally

CULTURE OF PROTOTYPING

Design Thinking involves embodied learning—learning to "think with your hands."

Prototypes can be anything from a storyboard, to a role play, to an actual physical object.

Prototypes of creative ideas are built as early as possible so the design team can learn just enough to generate useful feedback, determine an idea's strengths and weaknesses, and decide what new directions to pursue with more refined prototypes.

The important point is to learn by doing by giving form to an idea, evaluating it against other ideas, and ultimately improving upon it. "Fail early, fail often" is the motto, so prototyping is "quick, cheap, and dirty."

Make simple physical prototypes of your ideas as early as possible. Constantly test your ideas with people. Do not worry about making prototypes beautiful until you are sure that you have a resolved final design. Use the prototypes to guide and improve your design. Do a lot of low cost prototypes to test how your ideas physically work using cardboard, paper, markers, adhesive tape, photocopies, string and popsicle sticks. The idea is to test your idea, not to look like the final product. Expect to change it again. Limit your costs to ten or twenty dollars. Iterate, test and iterate. Do not make the prototype jewelry. It can stand in the way of finding the best design solution. In the minds of some a high fidelity prototype is a finished design solution rather than a tool for improving a design. You should make your idea physical as soon as possible. Be the first to get your hands dirty by making the idea real.

UNRECOGNIZED AND UNMET NEEDS

The methods of Design Thinking are capable of identifying and developing design solutions to meet human needs sometimes even before people know that they have needs. Testing prototypes with real people and observing their interactions and responses can lead designers to innovative solutions that are not yet recognized.

6 key principles that will ensure a design is user centered:
1. The design is based upon an explicit understanding of users, tasks and environments.
2. Users are involved throughout design and development.
3. The design is driven and refined by user-centered evaluation.
4. The process is iterative.
5. The design addresses the whole user experience.
6. The design team includes multidisciplinary skills and perspectives.

Some Questions to ask:
1. Who are the users?

2. What are the users' tasks and goals?
3. What are the users' experience levels?
4. What functions do the users need from the design?
5. What information will be needed by end-users?,
6. In what form do they need it?
7. How do users think the design should work?

CURIOUSITY

Curiosity is having an interest in the world. Curiosity is related to exploration, learning and innovation. Curiosity is one of the main driving forces behind human progress such as a caveman experimenting with fire.

High levels of curiosity in adults are connected to greater analytic ability, problem-solving skills and overall intelligence. Creativity is about exploring the unknown and curiosity can be the entry point into this exploration.

Children learn about the world through curiosity. A curious mind dives beneath the surface to understand the process. Curious people look at a challenge from multiple perspectives. Curious people find new paths to solutions.

The more exploration of the unknown, the more likely it will be that you will discover a new and better way of doing something. Curiosity allows a designer to make new connections and find inspiration in new places. The tools of Design Thinking such as observation methods, prototyping and interviewing allow curiosity to be applied in a systematic way. Curiosity helps create new insights which are the starting point for innovation.

FEEDBACK FROM STAKEHOLDERS AT EACH STAGE

Stakeholders include any individuals who are influence by the design. Specifically, the project team, end users, strategic partners, customers, alliances, vendors and senior management are project stakeholders

Possible stakeholders
1. Employees
2. Shareholders
3. Government
4. Customers
5. Suppliers
6. Prospective employees
7. Local communities
8. Global Community
9. Schools
10. Future generations
11. Ex-employees
12. Creditors
13. Professional associations
14. Competitors
15. Investors
16. Prospective customers
17. Communities

Why involve stakeholders? Stakeholder analysis helps to

identify:

1. Stakeholder interests
2. Ways to influence other stakeholders
3. Risks
4. Key people to be informed during the project
5. Negative stakeholders as well as their adverse effects on the project

HUMAN-CENTERED

Unlike the traditional approach to design, Design Thinking does not start with the technology or a product or a service. Design Thinking starts with the people who
need the product, process, or service and innovates for them.

Design Thinking identifies and addresses human needs. Design Thinking attempts to balance business requirements, human needs, the application of technologies and environmental sustainability.

Designers research how the end user has adapted their environment with their own designs or workarounds.

Human needs are investigated throughout the design process and the solution is refined through repetitive iterative steps with physical prototypes.

Design Thinking adapts the solution to the end user through understanding the end user.

OPTIMISM

Design Thinking is driven by the optimistic belief that we can create positive change. Creativity requires optimism, believing that all problems have a solution. A willingness to try new things, experiment, prototype, give up on old ideas or ways of doing things. It is a generative activity. The word is derived from the Latin word optimum, meaning "best." Being optimistic, means that you believe that you will discover the best possible solution to a design problem. To create anything new requires a belief that there is a better way. Some people will tell you why your idea will not work.

Some comments that kill optimism and progress:

1. We tried that before.
2. It costs too much
3. Let's get back to reality
4. That's not our problem
5. Now is not the right time.
6. It's impossible.
7. Quit dreaming.
8. We haven't got time for research
9. It's too radical
10. Let's put that one on the back burner for now.
11. We know what our customers want
12. I always follow my secretary's advice on color. She likes green.
13. I do not like the idea.
14. We are the experts
15. That's not my job.
16. We'll be a laughingstock
17. We've always done it this way

STORYTELLING

A powerful story can help ensure the success of a new product, service or experience. Storytelling can be an effective method of presenting a point of view. Research can uncover meaningful stories from end that illustrate needs or desires. These stories can become the basis of new designs or actions and be used to support decisions. Research shows that our attitudes, fears, hopes, and values are strongly influenced by story. Stories can be an effective way of communicating complex ideas and inspiring people to change.

How to tell an effective story

1. Answer in your story: What, why, when, who, where, how?
2. Offer a new vantage point
3. Share emotion
4. Communicate transformations
5. Communicate who you are.
6. Show cause and effect Describe conflicts and resolution.
7. Speak from your experience.
8. Describe how actions created change
9. Omit what is irrelevant.
10. Reveal meaning
11. Share your passion
12. Be honest and real
13. Build trust
14. Show connections
15. Transmits values
16. Share a vision
17. Share knowledge
18. Your story should differentiate you.
19. Use humor
20. Engage the audience
21. Craft the story for your audience.
22. Pose a problem and offer a resolution
23. The audience must be able to act on your story.

ACTIONS SPEAK LOADER THAN WORDS

Many companies today suffer from people who participate in discussion in meetings but do not follow through effectively with actions.

Design Thinking methods are focused on actions and creating real physical progress rather than discussion. Design Thinking is experiential and involved improvisation like a caveman experimenting with fire.

The process is continually hands on and means rolling your sleeves up and getting your hands dirty by trying things, making things and interacting rather than being a spectator.

Design Thinking deliberately takes an action oriented approach. This means that you should initiate physical actions yourself early in the project and continually as the project proceeds.

project, as successive versions, or iterations of a design are created.

Iterative design is the best approach when desiring to design products or systems that are user friendly and functional well.

The designer makes a prototype, tests and refines the design. The design improves from one iteration to the next and slowly eradicates use problems.

BUILD ITERATIONS

Iterative design will ensure a product or process is the best solution possible. When applied early in the development stage, significant cost savings are possible.

Other benefits to iterative design include:

1. Problems are discovered early when it is possible to fix them.
2. It involves end users so the solutions are real and relevant.
3. The designer focuses on those problems that are most relevant to the end user.
4. This approach enables the design team to continually improve the process.

BE VISUAL

Design Thinking is an effective approach for solving ambiguous, complex and changing problems. The solving of such problems often involves communicating ideas which are hard to describe in words. Visual mapping methods, images and sketches can help make complex ideas easier to understand and share.

You can use visual techniques even if you are not good at drawing. Take pictures of user interactions with your camera or phone. Explore some of the mapping methods described in the Methods chapter of this book. Use Venn diagrams, experience journeys, perceptual maps and radar charts to make information easier to comprehend. These visual methods are good ways of communicating connections and relationships.

CONTINUOUS LEARNING

Design Thinking is an ongoing learning process that seeks to incorporate the lessons learned into a continuous improvement of design. It incorporates ideas drawn from the Japanese management philosophy of Kaisen, Japanese for "improvement", or "change for the better" which focus upon continuous improvement of products and processes

INEXPENSIVE MISTAKES

Design Thinking makes successful designs by making mistakes early in inexpensive prototypes and learning through end user and stakeholder feedback. Prototypes are conceived and constructed in order to learn. We retain the features that are working and discover areas where the design can be improved. A process built around prototyping is an effective way of reaching an effective design solution in the most efficient way.

Designers must be willing to make mistakes in order to reach a successful solution. The environment should not punish exploration and iterative failures. Design Thinkers are searching for validity. They are problem solvers.
The price of failures rises as the project proceeds. It saves cost to fail early.

Abductive thinking which is the style of reasoning most likely to develop new innovative ideas and solutions makes reasonable assumptions based on incomplete information.

With this mode of thinking it is inevitable that some experiments directions will result in unexpected results. These unexpected results may be viewed as mistakes or as part of a learning process to find the best solution.

TOOLBOX

Design Thinking process is facilitated by a large number of design methods or tools.
The tools allow a designer to make informed design decisions that are not only about physical things but also about complex interfaces, systems, services and experiences. They will enable you to design products, systems buildings, interfaces and experiences with confidence that you have created the most informed design solutions for real people that is possible. These tools help designers think in four dimensions instead of three. .

The methods contained in this book will help you close the gap between your clients and organizations and the people that you are designing for to help you create more considered, informed, repeatable, innovative, empathetic design solutions that people need but may not yet know that they want. Different design practitioners can select different methods for their toolkit and apply them in different ways. There is no best combination.

EVIDENCE-BASED DESIGN

Design Thinking uses both intuitive and evidence based design. Evidence-Based Design is the process of basing design decisions on credible research to achieve the best possible outcomes. Evidence based design emphasizes the importance of basing decisions on the best possible data for the best possible outcomes

1. Evidence Based Design provides real evidence that improves outcomes and help with the clients bottom line.
2. The design is no longer based just on the designer's opinion
3. Define the problem that you are trying to solve.
4. Start with people. Identify the group of people that the design solution will be useful for.
5. Use an integrated multidisciplinary approach.
6. Use a human centric approach
7. Consider the business case and return on investment.
8. Design to measurable outcomes and to involve end users.
9. Use strategic partnerships to accelerate innovation,
10. Use simulation and testing to understand the end user's perspective
11. Communicate with and involve the stakeholders in the design process.

RE FRAMING THE PROBLEM

Reframe to create different perspectives and new ideas.

How to reframe:
1. Define the problem that you would like to address.
2. There is more than one way of looking at a problem. You could also define this problem in another way as."
3. What if a male or female used it?
4. What if it was used in China or Argentina?
5. "The underlying reason for the problem is."
6. "I think that the best solution is."
7. "You could compare this problem to the problem of."
8. "Another, different way of thinking about it is"

FUTURE ORIENTED

Design Thinking is a future oriented approach to designing. Most organizations base their new designs on what exists. Design Thinking allows an organization to change for the better. It allows an organization to move from being a follower to being a leader in the market.

"

Empathy is key. It's not about you. You need the ability to understand and share the feelings of others.

PIETER BAERT
Service consultant

EVERYONE CAN CONTRIBUTE

Design Thinking process involves many stakeholders in working together to find a balanced design solution. The designer is a member of the orchestra. The customer is involved throughout the design process and works with the design team to communicate their needs and desires and to help generate design solutions that are relevant to them.

The many methods used help the design team to understand the diverse perspectives of the many stakeholders. It takes some courage for a designer to listen and recognize the point of view of the stakeholders. Managers, designers, social scientists, engineers marketers, stakeholders and others collaborate creatively to design.

The process is one of co-creation and the designer is a listener and a facilitator. Everyone adds value to the design. Design Thinking is not just for professional designers. Everyone can contribute. Many schools are now teaching Design Thinking to children as an approach that can be applied to life.

WICKED PROBLEMS

Design Thinking focuses on solutions to problems, It may be better than traditional design processes at addressing what have been called "Wicked Problems". Wicked problems are ill-defined or tricky problems, not necessarily wicked in the sense of evil. The iterative prototype and testing based approach does not assume a solution from the outset but experiments and tries alternative solutions and proceeds to refine the designs on the basis of successful testing.

Super wicked problems

K. Levin, proposed an additional type of problem called the "super wicked problem"He defined super wicked problems as having the following additional characteristics:
1. There is limited time.
2. No central decision maker.
3. The people who are trying to solve a problem are the same people who are causing the problem.
4. Policies discount the future irrationally.

Rittel and Webber specified ten characteristics of wicked problems in 1973:
1. "There is no definitive formulation of a wicked problem
2. Wicked problems have no stopping rule.
3. Solutions to wicked problems are not true-or-false, but better or worse.
4. There is no immediate and no ultimate test of a solution to a wicked problem.
5. Wicked problems do not have

an enumerable set of potential solutions,

6. Every wicked problem is essentially unique.
7. Every wicked problem can be considered to be a symptom of another problem.
8. The existence of a discrepancy representing a wicked problem can be explained in numerous ways. The choice of explanation determines the nature of the problem's resolution.
9. The planner has no right to be wrong
10. Wicked problems have no given alternative solutions."

Source: Rittel and Webber

ANALOGOUS SITUATIONS

"Bring your staff together in a large room and put up a big white board. Create two columns, one for emotions and activities involved in your customer experience and a second one for similar situations which incorporate the same emotions and activities. Once you start filling in the first column, people will naturally start to brainstorm the analogous situations. When those are noted on the white board, people will start adding new emotions and activities to the first column based on their own experiences with the analogous situations. At the end of the process, choose the most vital pain points and use them as the basis of a brainstorming session to look for solutions and methods of improving the overall customer experience."

Source : http://blog.triode.ca

FOCUS ON PEOPLE

Design is about people than it is about things. Stand in those people's shoes, see through their eyes, uncover their stories, share their worlds. Start each design by identifying a problem that real people are experiencing. Use the methods in this book selectively to gain empathy, understanding, and to inform your design. Good process is not a substitute for talented, motivated and skilled people on your design team.

GET PHYSICAL

Make simple physical prototypes of your ideas as early as possible. Constantly test your ideas with people. Do not worry about making prototypes beautiful until you are sure that you have a resolved design direction. Use the prototypes to guide and improve your design. Do several low cost prototypes to test how your Ideas physically work.. using cardboard, paper, markers, adhesive tape, photocopies, string and popsicle sticks. The idea is to test your idea, not to look like the final product. Expect to change it again. Limit your costs to ten or twenty dollars. Iterate, test and iterate. Do not make the prototype jewelry. It can stand in the way of finding the best design solution. In

TAKE CONSIDERED RISKS

Taking considered risks helps create differentiated design. Many designers and organizations do not have the flexibility or courage to create innovative, differentiated design solutions so they create products and services that are like existing products and services and compete on price.

USE THE TOOLS

To understand the point of view of diverse peoples and cultures a designer needs to connect with those people and their context. The tools in this book will help you see the world through the eyes of those people.

LEARN TO SEE AND HEAR

Reach out to understand people. Interpret what you see and hear. Read between the lines. Make new connections between the things you see and hear.

COMBINE ANALYTICAL AND CREATIVE THINKING

Effective collaboration is part of effective design. Designers work like members of an orchestra. We need to work with managers, engineers, salespeople and other professions. Human diversity and life experience contribute to better design solutions.

LOOK FOR BALANCE

Design Thinking seeks a balance of design factors including:
1. Business.
2. Empathy with people.
3. Application OF technology.
4. Environmental consideration.

TEAM COLLABORATION

Design today is a more complex activity than it was in the past. Business, technology, global cultural issues, environmental considerations, and human considerations all need careful consideration. Design Thinking recognizes the need for designers to be working as members of multidisciplinary multi skilled teams.

REPEATABLE INNOVATION

a 2015 study found that in 69% of companies interviewed considered that applying the Design Thinking process and methods had made their innovation more efficient. This study was the first large scale study of the innovation effect of implementing Design Thinking.

Data from 2015 study by Hasso-Plattner-Institut für softwaresystemtechnik an der Universität Potsdam, September 2015 of 235 German and international companies of all sizes

"

The secret to
collaboration is finding
a rhythm that alternates
between team creativity
and individual creativity.

MARTIN NEUMEIER

American author who writes on the topics of brand, design,
innovation, and creativity

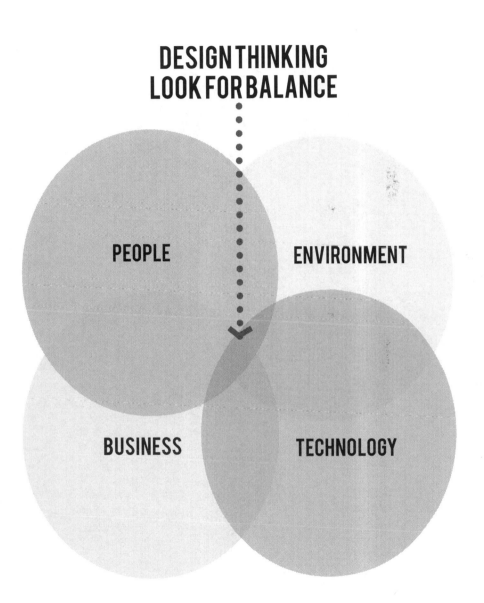

DESIGN THINKING
LOOK FOR BALANCE

PEOPLE

ENVIRONMENT

BUSINESS

TECHNOLOGY

DESIGN THINKING CASE STUDIES

"

Good design begins
with honesty, asks
tough questions and
comes from collaboration
and from trusting your
intuition

FREEMAN THOMAS
Automotive designer

SOME ORGANIZATIONS LEARNING AND APPLYING DESIGN THINKING

3M
Accenture
AdaptAir
Adobe
Ahold
AirBnB
Airbus
Amway
ANZ Bank
Center for Entrepreneurial Leadership at African Leadership Academy
Apple
Arup
Australian Taxation Office
AutoDesk
Bank of America: Keep the Change
Bayer
Bayteq
BBVA Bancomer
Bertelsmann
BMW
Bristol Maids
Celfinet
CERN IdeaLab
Charité Berlin, BCRT/BSRT, Biothinking Program
Charité: Onkolizer
Chick-fil-a
Cincinnati Children's Hospital Medical Center
Cisco
Citrix
Clorox Company
Condair: JS Humidifiers
Creuznacher

D.Light
Daimler
Datascope Analytics
Deloitte digital
Deloitte Innovation
Derdack
Deutsche Bahn
Deutsche Bank
DHL
D-Lab: Charcoal
D-Rev: ReMotions's JaipurKnee
EBS Business School
Electrolux: Design Lab
Embrace Infant Incubator
Everest
Flad Architects
Fraport
Future Balloons
FutureGov
GE
GE: GE Adventure Series
GE: Healthcare
Georgia Tech
GlaxoSmithKline
Godrej: Chotu Kool
Google: Google Ventures
GoPro
IBM
IKB Innsbrucker Kommunal Betriebe
IKEA + IDEO
Infosys
Intuit Inc.
Israel Palestine Center for Research
Janssen-Cilag
JetBlue
JLL-Jones Lang LaSalle

Juntos Finanzas
Kaiser Permanente
Kickstart
Lambeth Council
Mappy
Marriot 4 Seasons
Mattel: Platypus
Mayo Clinics
Metro AG
Metropolitan Group
MeYouHealth
Microsoft
Miele
Miraclefeet Brace
Nasdaq
Naval Undersea Warfare Center
(NUWC) Newport
Nestle?
New York Times
NIKE
Novabase
Onclaude
P&G
P&G früher)/ Blackberry
P&G: Consumer Products: Swiffer
Panasonic: Oxyride
PepsiCo
Pfizer: Nicorette
Philips Electronics (PHG)
Pillpack
Ploom
Pulse
Pulse
PwC Australia
RadBoud REshape
Ravel
San Francisco's Department of

Emergency Management
SAP
SAP CSR + Sankara eye care
Schröder und Partner
Sennheiser
Sense Consulting Ltd. Croatia
Shell Innovation Research
Shimano
Siemens
St. Joseph Health
Stanley Works: Black & Decker
Stcelcase
Sternin Positive Deviance Initiative
SunCorp
Swisscom
Telekom
THALES
The Australian Center for Social
Innovation
The Good Kitchen
Three Twins Organic Ice Cream
Toyota
Unilever
University of Pittsburgh Medical
Center
US - Presidential Innovation
Fellows Program
VF Corporation
VisioSpring
Vlisco
VW
Whirlpool
WikiMedia
Xing
ZOO Hannover

CASE STUDIES

PEPSI

PepsiCo is the latest company to come out in support of "Design Thinking" and to make a case for investment in design. In the September 2015 issue of the Harvard Business Review, PepsiCo CEO Indra Nooyi describes using Design Thinking to "rethink the entire experience, from conception to what's on the shelf to the post-product experience." Nooyi describes that, although early days, she believes her approach has "delivered great shareholder value while strengthening the company for the long term."

"First, I gave each of my direct reports an empty photo album and a camera. I asked them to take pictures of anything they thought represented good design. After six weeks, only a few people returned the albums. Some had their wives take pictures. Many did nothing at all. They didn't know what design was"

For companies like PepsiCo, encouraging, and even mandating, a perspective that insists on customer experience and empathy can lead to richer insights, more on-point products and clearer strategies to deliver them by helping brands connect to what customers find compelling.

Source: brandchannel.com

AIRBNB

In 2009, Airbnb was close to going bust. Like so many startups, they had launched but barely anyone noticed. The company's revenue was flatlined at $200 per week. Split between three young founders living in San Francisco, this meant near indefinite losses on zero growth.

The two founders who had design backgrounds decided to reinvent the company using Design Thinking. A little over a year later the company had a billion dollar turnover.

AirBnB's Head of User Research (2012-2014)
""having designer founders and being design-centered from day one makes you [as an organization] pay attention to those details. ... A lot of Design Thinking is about being creative [but it is also] about looking at what we know and triangulating information that we have and having that inspire creativity.""

"There are engineers who care about their engineering problems and maybe the users are less relevant. We just don't hire these kind of engineers here. Every engineer cares about the user and has a respect for design"

ERICSSON

Ericsson apply Design Thinking process and methods through Innova, a startup incubator within the company to assess existing ideas and turn them into marketable concepts.

"It was one unit introducing Design Thinking in their organizational structure and it became an innovation practice. A practice that they now share with the whole company."

Innova aims to support an entrepreneurial spirit amongst Ericsson's employees. After its third year, the Innova platform had 6.000 users. More than 4.000 ideas were submitted to the platform, with more than 450 ideas receiving first round funding and 45 receiving second round funding.

Source : thisisdesignthinking.net

SINGAPORE GOVERNMENT

The Ministry of Manpower's Work Pass Division used Design Thinking to develop better ways to support foreigners who choose Singapore as a destination to live, work and set up businesses.

Design Thinking methods were applied. Work Pass Division began to consider services through the eyes of their users the employers, employment agencies and foreign workers.

Between 2005 and 2009, the EPOL was redesigned to increase the information flow to users of the system. This has helped to shift the perception of WPD from a high-handed regulator to a responsive and transparent facilitator of employment.

PROCTOR & GAMBLE

Clay Street Project @ Procter & GambleIn 2004, Procter & Gamble (P&G) established an internal innovation pro-gram, which incorporated Design Thinking. In the program teams from multiple disciplines and units within P&G gather for a period of 10 to 12 weeks to develop user-centered solutions. Since Clay Street produced numerous internal success stories P&G decided to provide their setup as a service for other business partners. The oferings range from one-day workshops to project support over a period of several weeks. The Clay Street initiative and a Design Thinking Network now serve as a foundation to spread Design Thinking in the organization.

http://www.theclaystreetproject.com

INTUIT

Design for Delight (D4D) Design Thinking program was established in 2007. Its mandate is to foster more entrepreneurial behavior throughout the whole organization. So far, over 200 innovation catalysts have been trained and support teams from multiple disciplines in the design of financial service experiences for Intuit's customers. They are allowed to dedicate a minimum of ten percent of their working time to training and helping others in their projects. Catalysts were enabled by a massive internal change program, which integrated a redefinition of the company's core values and major changes into the spatial working environments.

http://intuitlabs.com

PULSE

Ankit and Akshay develop Pulse with Design Thinking and empathy. They took a 10 week class called launchpad course at the d school at Stanford where rule number one is start with empathy. Students must start a business and have customers by week 5. Students must talk to customers from day one.

Ankit had a software company in india before coming to the United States. He says that we never talked to a customer and as a result we never had a customer. To develop the class project they set up shop in a coffee shop in Palo Alto for ten hours a day for several weeks. They are not allowed back there.

They see everyone reading a newspaper so decide to do a news aggregator for iPad.At first they used post it notes because they had no software.First week everyone did not like it by week 3 everyone asking whether it shipped with the iPad. They made 100 changes a day based on customer feedback.

At Ian iPad developers conference Steve jobs showed an iPad with their software. Pulse had soon developed 20 million users and Linkedin bought their company for 90 million dollars

IBM

"Mr. Gilbert and his team talk a lot about "iteration cycles," "lateral thinking," "user journeys" and "empathy maps." To the uninitiated, the canons of Design Thinking can sound mushy and self-evident. But across corporate America, there is a rising enthusiasm for Design Thinking not only to develop products but also to guide strategy and shape decisions of all kinds. The September cover article of the Harvard Business Review was "The Evolution of Design Thinking." Venture capital firms are hiring design experts, and so are companies in many industries.

The computing giant has discovered "Design Thinking," the product-development technique that puts customers first on the way to creating goods and services. Lohr writes that IBM plans to hire 1,100 designers across the company by year-end, on a path to employing 1,500. The goal is to have their methods infuse every aspect of how IBM does business

Asked what she tells anxious large shareholders, Ms. Rometty replied that "the key message" is that IBM is the only technology company that is more than a century old because it has reinvented itself repeatedly in the past, and it is doing so again today.."

Soruce New York times November 14 2015

INFOSYS

30,000 Infosys staff to be trained on Design Thinking

MUMBAI: Infosys has already signed up 22 customers on its Design Thinking offering and will train 30,000 of its employees on Design Thinking by the end of the year to further boost growth in that consultancy service, chief executive officer Vishal Sikka said. Sikka has been pushing Design Thinking as the cornerstone of his plan to help the company grow. The company has also trained 250 of its top executives and its sales teams on Design Thinking.

""With Design Thinking, we should be able to identify problems and not just solve them for customers that are pointed out to us. No one is doing this sort of consultancy in a big way," Sikka said

Design Thinking is also a way for the company to win deals focused on new digital technologies, that are likely to help the company in the rebid market, he said.

Source: Times of India

SIEMENS CT CHINA

Siemens has developed the program "Industrial Design Thinking in China (i.DT)" to train the creativity of Research & Development teams through real projects for need driven innovation with disruptive potential. The i.DT lab ran in the spring of 2015, with large workshop room, several dedicated project rooms, and an advanced machine shop with 3D printer, Computerized Numerical Control (CNC) and laser cutter to take the low resolution prototypes to the next professional level.

The process of i.DT, which can last for several months and include a number of workshops, starts from the definition of the innovation target and ends with a sales pitch. It uses extreme users and low resolution prototypes as stimuli, to satisfy unmet needs by integrating multiple technologies or businesses through fast iterations of needfinding, brainstorming, prototyping, and testing. The method has been successfully used in China for the past three years, in more than 20 development projects to date. Now i.DT is also coming to Germany to support business.

Source: Siemens Press release 2015

GE HEALTHCARE

The challenge was how to create a more child friendly CT, X-Ray and MRI scanning experience.

Diagnostic imaging procedures are an unpleasant experience for patients. Doug Dietz is an industrial designer, working for GE healthcare since more than 20 years. He saw a little girl who was crying on her way to a scanner that was designed by him. Doug Dietz tried to find inspiration for this project through Design Thinking. "I started to imagine how powerful this tool could be if I brought it back and got cross-functional teams to work together." He started by observing and gaining empathy for young children at a day care center. Next, he created the first prototype of what would become the "Adventure Series" scanner and was able to get it installed as a pilot program in the children's hospital at the University of Pittsburgh Medical Center."

The patient satisfaction scores went up 90 percent. Children do not suffer of anxiety anymore. Instead some of them even ask their parents if they can come back tomorrow.

EMBRACE

Students at the Stanford d. school were challenged to design a less expensive incubator for babies born prematurely in Nepal. The students traveled to Nepal to meet with families and doctors and see the problem for themselves.

Based on the data collected, the design team reframes the design problem.

They used pictures, videos and storytelling of their experiences to brainstorm solutions. The students who undertook this project didn't stop with a prototype. They formed a company called Embrace and started manufacturing the product, which sells for $25. Embrace now has programs in 11 different countries and has helped over 50,000 premature and low birth weight infants. And all it started with the Design Thinking process. It has estimated that the product has saved 20,000 lives.

It has been so successful that the product is being purchased by US health providers where the cost of incubation using traditional methods in hospitals may be more than $100,000 per child.

Source: http://blog.triode.ca/

RESEARCH
EMPATHIZE
DISCOVER

"

Develop a deep understanding of your end-users through engaging them observing and listening to them explain their point of view, their problems and their needs.

This phase involves both creative and analytical thinking

"

Innovation is all about people. Innovation thrives when the population is diverse, accepting and willing to cooperate.

VIVEK WADHWA
Entrepreneur Researcher and Writer.

ASSEMBLE YOUR TEAM

Select a diverse cross disciplinary group of people. Have different disciplines, different genders, ages, cultures, represented for the most successful results. Have some T   shaped people. These are people who have more than one area of experience or training such as design and management. They wilk help your team collaborate productively.

DEFINE YOUR TARGET AUDIENCE

Creating a projected user models will keep the development team rooted to a realistic user requirements and minimizes user frustration with the real product. Having a deep understanding of users can help development team better understand the wants & needs of the targeted customers. This will help the development team relate better with the target user. Understanding user tasks helps in developing design solutions that will ensure that the user expectations are met & avoid design errors and customer frustration. Use research methods such as interviewing, observation, empathy maps and user experience maps to better understand your audience. Market segmentation is basically the division of market into smaller segments. It helps identify potential customers and target them.

Types of segmentation
1.   Behavior segmentation
2.   Benefit segmentation
3.   Psychographic segmentation
4.   Geographic segmentation
5.   Demographic segmentation

1.   What is your target group's goals emotions, experiences, needs and desires?
2.   Information collected from just a few people is unlikely to be representative of the whole range of users.
3.   What are the user tasks and activities?
4.   How will the user use the product or service to perform a task?
5.   What is the context of the user?
6.   Where are they? What surrounds them physically and virtually or culturally?
7.   How large is your user group?

When defining your target audience consider factors such as:
1.   Age
2.   Gender
3.   Occupation
4.   Industry
5.   Travel
6.   Citizenship status
7.   Marital state
8.   Income
9.   Culture
10. Occupation
11. Language
12. Religion
13. Location
14. Education
15. Nationality
16. Mobility
17. Migration
18. Mental state
19. Abilities
20. Disabilities
21. Health

TEAM BUILDING EXERCISE

A team building exercise is a short exercise at the beginning of a Design Thinking project that helps the design team work productively together as quickly as possible. The duration of an exercise is usually less than 30 minutes. I describe some examples of exercises in the following chapter.

They are an important component of collaborative or team based design. The Design Thinking approach recognizes the value of designers working productively as members of a diverse cross-disciplinary teams with managers, engineers, marketers and other professionals.

SHARE WHAT YOU KNOW

1. In the project kick off meeting ask every team member to introduce themselves and to describe in 3 minutes what experience they have that may be relevant to the project.
2. The moderator can list areas of knowledge on a white board.

IDENTIFY WHAT YOU NEED TO KNOW

Arrange a project kick-off meeting. Invite your team and important stakeholders. On a white board or flip chart create two lists.
Ask each person to introduce themselves and describe what they know or have experienced that may be useful for implementing the project. Brainstorm with your group the areas that are unknown and how that information may be obtained. Formulate a research plan and assign responsibilities, tasks and deliverables with dates.

UNCOVER NEEDS

1. "What causes the problem?"
2. "What are the impacts of the problem?"
3. ""What are possible solutions?"
4. Probe about workarounds How do people adapt their environment to solve problems that they have?
5. Ask what their single biggest obstacle is to achieve what they are trying to achieve How can you help them?
6. Ask what's changing in their world What are the trends?
7. Observe people
8. Can you see problems they have that they perhaps do not even recognize are problems?
9. Ask other stakeholders

DEFINE THE GOALS

A goal is the intent or intents of the design process.

1. Write a detailed description of the design problem.
2. Define a list of needs that are connected to the design problem.
3. Make a list of obstacles that need to be overcome to solve the design problem.
4. Make a list of constraints that apply to the problem.
5. Rewrite the problem statement to articulate the above requirements.

UNCOVER PEOPLES STORIES

A powerful story can help ensure the success of a new product, service or experience. Storytelling can be an effective method of presenting a point of view. Research can uncover meaningful stories from end that illustrate needs or desires. These stories can become the basis of new designs or actions and be used to support decisions. Stories can be an effective way of communicating complex ideas and inspiring people to change.

1. The stories help to get buy-in from people throughout the design process and may be used to help sell a final design.
2. Real life stories are persuasive.
3. They are different to advertising because they are able to influence a design if uncovered from users during the early research phases and provide authenticity.

Challenges
1. A story with too much jargon will lose an audience.
2. Not everyone has the ability to tell vivid stories.
3. Stories are not always generalizable.

An effective story:
1. Meets information needs for your audience
2. Offer a new vantage point
3. Tell real world stories
4. Evoke the future
5. Share emotion
6. Communicate transformations
7. Communicate who you are.
8. Describe actions
9. Show cause and effect
10. Speak from your experience.
11. Describe how actions created change
12. Omit what is irrelevant.
13. Share your passion
14. Be honest and real
15. Build trust
16. Transmits values
17. Share a vision
18. Share knowledge
19. Your story should differentiate you.
20. Use humor
21. Engage the audience
22. Craft the story for your audience.
23. Pose a problem and offer a resolution
24. Use striking imagery
25. The audience must be able to act on your story.

"

For good ideas
and true innovation,
you need human
interaction, conflict,
argument, debate

MARGARET HEFFERNAN
CEO businessperson and writer

INNOVATION DIAGNOSTIC

WHAT IS IT?

An innovation diagnostic is an evaluation of an organization's innovation capabilities. It reviews practices by stakeholders which may help or hinder innovation. An innovation diagnostic is the first step in preparing an implementing a strategy to create an organizational culture that supports innovation.

WHY USE THIS METHOD?

1. It helps organizations develop sustainable competitive advantage.
2. Helps identify innovation opportunities
3. Helps develop innovation strategy.

WHEN TO USE THIS METHOD

1. Know Context
2. Know User
3. Frame insights
4. Explore Concepts
5. Make Plans

HOW TO USE THIS METHOD

An innovation diagnostic reviews organizational and stakeholder practices using both qualitative and quantitative methods including

1. The design and development process
2. Strategic practices and planning.
3. The ability of an organization to monitor and respond to relevant trends.
4. Technologies
5. Organizational flexibility
6. Ability to innovate repeatedly and consistently

INNOVATION DIAGNOSTIC TEST

DOES MANAGEMENT COMMUNICATE THE NEED FOR INNOVATION?

1. There is no innovation in our organization
2. Innovation is not a high priority
3. Our managers sometimes talk about innovation
4. Our managers discuss innovation but not why it is needed
5. Managers regularly state the compelling need for innovation

WHAT IS YOUR ORGANIZATIONAL STRATEGY?

1. We make low cost goods or services
2. Efficient operations
3. We are a customer focused organization
4. Fast Follower
5. Market leaders

IS THE BUSINESS THAT YOU ARE IN UNDERSTOOD BY EMPLOYEES?

1. We are not sure
2. We may get different answers from different managers
3. The definition changes in
4. We have some clarity

5. We are very clear about what business we are in

IS YOUR ORGANIZATION INNOVATIVE?

1. No
2. Probably not
3. We would like to be
4. There is some innovation
5. We are clearly an innovative organization

HOW DOES YOUR COMPANY INNOVATE?

1. We react to market forces without innovation
2. There is little innovation
3. We do some incremental innovation
4. We do mainly incremental innovation but would like to do some breakthrough innovation
5. We manage a portfolio of incremental and more substantial innovation and manage risks

DOES YOUR MANAGEMENT SUPPORT INNOVATION?

1. No
2. No resources are allocated to innovation

3. Some resources are allocated
4. We have some resources and some involvement from managers in innovation
5. We have clearly defined resources allocated and senior management is actively involved in planning and managing innovation

DO YOU HAVE CROSS DISCIPLINARY DESIGN TEAMS?

1. Never
2. Rarely
3. Sometimes
4. Usually
5. Always

DO YOU USE OUTSIDE EXPERTS TO ASSIST IN YOUR INNOVATION PROCESS?

1. Never
2. Rarely
3. Sometimes
4. Usually
5. Always

HOW OFTEN DOES YOUR ORGANIZATION ENGAGE CUSTOMERS TO IDENTIFY THEIR UNMET NEEDS?

1. Never
2. Rarely
3. Sometimes
4. Usually
5. Always

HOW WOULD YOU DEFINE THE RISK TOLERANCE AT YOUR COMPANY?

1. We don't take any risks
2. We rarely take risks
3. Sometimes we take substantial risks
4. We manage our risk portfolio actively and take big risks when appropriate.

HOW ARE NEW IDEAS RECEIVED IN YOUR ORGANIZATION?

1. We fire people with new ideas
2. We rarely adopt new ideas
3. We sometimes adopt new ideas but they are mostly not considered
4. We regularly consider new ideas
5. We actively generate and adopt new ideas

Add up the numbers of each answer that you selected and calculate a total for all the questions

HOW WELL DID YOU SCORE?

SCORE 35 TO 45
HIGHLY INNOVATIVE ORGANIZATION

The highest level of innovation is where companies are able to create innovations that change how people live. The highest level of innovation also brings the highest level of risk, as many times this level of innovation involves products or services that no one has thought of and customers do not know they want. Revolutionary products and services, large investment, big risks high payoff

SCORE 25 TO 35
INNOVATIVE ORGANIZATION

The third level is the beginning of large financial and product risk, but it is also where the rewards are potentially larger. This level also requires that the business devote resources to monitoring progress and actively assessing risk throughout the development process. Evolutionary products, large investment, medium risk, some payoff

SCORE 15 TO 25
SOMEWHAT INNOVATIVE

The second level is a higher level of changes. Level Two changes include integrating new features into existing products on the market or creating differentiated versions of the same new product to sell to various demographic groups. These new features require what can be considered a medium level of investment and risk. Advancement of existing products medium investment and risk medium payoff

SCORE 0 TO 15
LOW INNOVATION

The first level emphasizes minimal changes to existing products, a low amount of new investment, and very low risk. Examples at this level would be changing the color of a product or putting a new logo design on a label. Essentially all companies are capable of achieving this level, as it does not require unique skills. Few new features on existing products, low investment and risk. Low payoff.

PATIENT STAKEHOLDER MAP

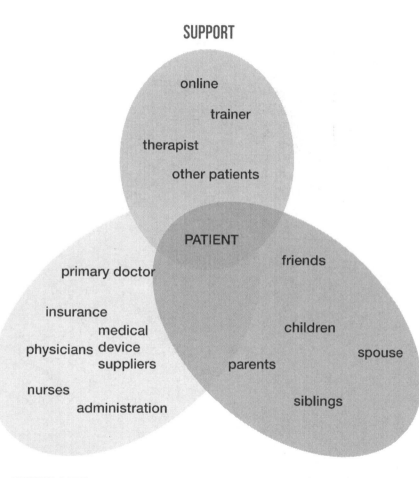

SUPPORT

online

trainer

therapist

other patients

PATIENT

friends

primary doctor

insurance

medical

physicians device

suppliers

children

spouse

parents

nurses

siblings

administration

HEALTH CARE

FAMILY & FRIENDS

STAKEHOLDER MAPS

WHAT IS IT

Stakeholders maps are used to document the key stakeholders and their relationship.

At the beginning of a design project it is important to identify the key stakeholders and their relationships. The map serves as a reference for the design team.

WHO INVENTED IT

Mitchell 1997

WHY USE THIS METHOD

1. Stakeholder mapping helps discover ways to influence other stakeholders.
2. Stakeholder mapping helps discover risks.
3. Stakeholder mapping helps discover positive stakeholders to involve in the design process.

CHALLENGES?

Stakeholder mapping helps discover negative stakeholders and their associated risks.

HOW TO USE THIS METHOD

1. Invite six known stakeholders to a meeting.
2. Give each stakeholder a block of post it notes.
3. Brainstorm with the group additional stakeholders
4. Cluster stockholders into relevant groups
5. Assign priorities for individual stakeholders based on the value of their potential feedback during the design process,
6. Map the stakeholders.
7. Can initially be documented on a white board, cards, post-it-notes and consolidated as a diagram through several iterations showing hierarchy and relationships.

"

I keep six honest serving men. They taught me all I knew Their names are what and why and when and how and where and who

RUDYARD KIPLING
English short-story writer, poet, and novelist

WWWWWH

WHAT IS IT?

'Who, What, Where, When, Why, and How'?
is a method for getting a thorough understanding of the problem, It is used to obtain basic information in police investigations. A well known golden rule of journalism is that if you want to know the full story about something you have to answer all the five W's. Journalists argue your story isn't complete until you answer all six questions.

1. Who is involved?
2. What occurred?
3. When did it happen?
4. Where did it happen?
5. Why did it occur?

WHO INVENTED IT?

Hermagoras of Temnos, Greece 1st century BC.

WHY USE THIS METHOD?

This method helps create a story that communicates clearly the nature of an activity or event to stakeholders.

CHALLENGES

1. The answers may be subjective.

WHEN TO USE THIS METHOD

1. Define intent
2. Know Context
3. Know User
4. Frame insights

HOW TO USE THIS METHOD

1. Ask the questions starting with the 5 w's and 1 h question words.
2. Identify the people involved
3. Identify the activities and make a list of them.
4. Identify all the places and make a list of them.
5. Identify all the time factors and make a list of them.
6. Identify causes for events of actions and make a list of them.
7. Identify the way events took place and make a list of them.
8. Study the relationships between the information.

RESOURCES

Pen
Paper

"

You start from what people, users, customers, consumers need or want their motivations and the problems they are trying to solve.

PIETER BAERT
Service consultant

FIVE WHYS

WHAT IS IT
Five Whys is an iterative question method used to discover the under-lying cause of a problem. For every effect there is a root cause. The primary goal of the technique is to determine the underlying cause of a problem by repeating the question "Why?"

WHO INVENTED IT
The technique was originally developed by Sachichi Toyoda Sakichi Toyoda was a Japanese inventor and industrialist. He was born in Kosai, Shizuoka. The son of a poor carpenter, Toyoda is referred to as the "King of Japanese Inventors". He was the founder of the Toyota Motor company. The method is still an important part of Toyota training, culture and success.

WHY USE THIS METHOD
1. When we fix the root cause the problem does not reoccur

HOW TO USE THIS METHOD
1. Five whys could be taken further to a sixth, seventh, or higher level, but five is generally sufficient to get to a root cause.
2. Gather a team and develop the problem statement in agreement
3. Establish the time and place that the problem is occurring
4. Ask the first "why" of the team: why is this problem taking place?
5. Ask four more successive "whys," repeating the process
6. You will have identified the root cause when asking "why" yields no further useful information.
7. Discuss the last answers and settle on the most likely systemic cause.
8. Fix the root problem

EMPATHY MAPS

WHAT IS IT?

A mapping method that analyses each part of a user experience.. An Empathy Map gives a high level view of where an experience is good or bad. Used to improve a user experience.

The biggest single cause of failure of new products and services in the marketplace is that the organization creating the product or service did not understand completely the customer's perspective. This method helps draw out the main components of the customer experience so that problems can be identified and fixed.

Empathy Map is a tool that helps the design team empathize with people they are designing for. You can create an empathy map for a group of customers or a persona.

WHO INVENTED IT?

Scott Matthews and Dave Gray at PLANE now Dachis Group.

HOW LONG DOES IT TAKE?

One to three hours per persona.

WHY USE THIS METHOD?

This tool helps a design team understand the customers and their context. It is an outside in technique.

CHALLENGES

1. Emotions must be inferred by observing clues.
2. This method does not provide the same level of rigor as traditional personas but requires less investment.

WHEN TO USE THIS METHOD

1. Know Context
2. Know User
3. Frame insights

RESOURCES

1. Empathy map template
2. White board
3. or blackboard
4. or video projector
5. or Large sheet of paper
6. Dry-erase markers
7. Post-it-notes
8. Pens
9. Video Camera

HOW TO USE THIS METHOD

1. A team of 4 to 12 people is a good number for this method.
2. The best people to involve are people who have direct interaction with customers.
3. The team should represent various functions in your organization such as management, design, marketing, sales, and engineering. It is helpful to also include some stakeholders such as customers and others affected by the end design. The process will help draw out useful information from them.
4. This method can be used with personas.
5. The map should be based on real information from customers. This can be gathered from sources such as interviews, observation, web analytics, customer service departments and focus groups.
6. Segment your market then create a persona representing an average customer in each segment. Four to six personas are a good number.
7. Draw a circle to represent your target persona.
8. Divide the circle into sections

that represent aspects of that personss's sensory experience. It is common to have boxes for seeing and hearing. Some experiences such as drinking coffee could include boxes for other senses such as taste and smell.

9. Place two boxes at the bottom of the map and label them "Pain" and "Gain".
10. Ask your team to describe from the persona's point of view their experience.
11. Populate the map by taking note of the following traits of your user as you review your notes, audio, and video from your fieldwork: What are they thinking, feeling, saying, doing, hearing, seeing?
12. Fill in the diagram with real, tangible, sensory experiences.
13. Once you have filled all of the top boxes move the post it notes for negative components of the experience into the lower pain box and positive into the gain box.
14. The pain box can serve as a start for identifying the problems to fix in the ideation phase.

HOW TO CREATE AN EMPATHY MAP

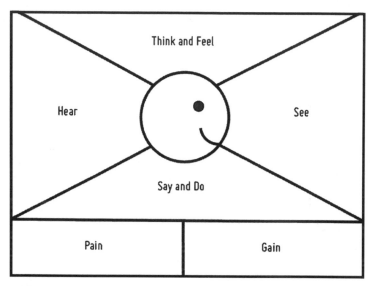

1 Create the Empathy Map template on a white board, on a large sheet of paper or project it on a wall.

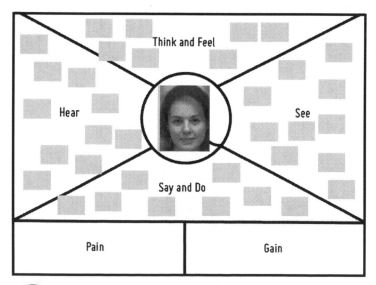

3 Populate top four boxes one at a time. You can have more than four boxes in the top section if for example smell and touch are important for your persona's experience.

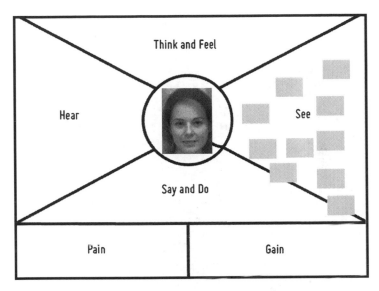

2 Populate one box with post it notes based on your research on the particular persona

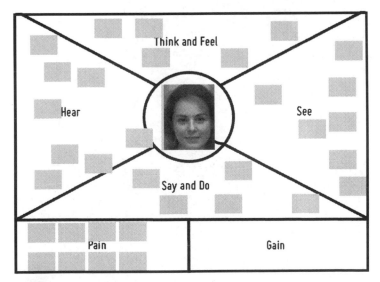

4 Move the negative experiences into the pain box. Move the positive experiences into the gain box. The pain box can be the basis for experiential problems to fix in the ideation phase.

INTERVIEWING

WHAT IS IT?

Interviewing is a method of ethnographic research that has been described as a conversation with a purpose.

WHY USE THIS METHOD?

1. Contextual interviews uncover tacit knowledge about people's context.
2. The information gathered can be detailed.
3. The information produced by contextual inquiry is relatively reliable

CHALLENGES

1. End users may not have the answers
2. Contextual inquiry may be difficult to challenge even if it is misleading.
3. Keep control
4. Be prepared
5. Be aware of bias
6. Be neutral
7. Select location carefully

RESOURCES

Computer
Notebook
Pens
Video camera
Release forms
Interview plan or structure
Questions, tasks and discussion items
Confidentiality agreement

WHEN TO USE THIS METHOD

1. Know Context
2. Know User
3. Frame insights

HOW TO USE THIS METHOD

1. Contextual inquiry may be structured as 2 hour one on one interviews.
2. The researcher does not usually impose tasks on the user.
3. Go to the user's context. Talk, watch listen and observe.
4. Understand likes and dislikes.
5. Collect stories and insights.
6. See the world from the user's point of view.
7. Take permission to conduct interviews.
8. Do one-on-one interviews.
9. The researcher listens to the user.
10. 2 to 3 researchers conduct an interview.
11. Understand relationship between people, product and context.
12. Document with video, audio and notes.

INTERVIEW GUIDE

HOW TO USE THIS METHOD

1. Plan in advance what you want to achieve
2. Research the topic
3. Select a person to interview.
4. Meet them in their location if possible.
5. Set a place, date, and time.
6. Be sure he or she understands how long the interview should take and that you plan to record the session.
7. Start with an open-ended question. It is a good way to put the candidate at ease,
8. Tape record the interview if possible.
9. Decide what information you need
10. Write down the information you'd like to collect through the interview. Now frame your interview questions around this information.
11. Prepare follow-up questions to ask.
12. Research the person that you are interviewing
13. Check your equipment and run through your questions.
14.
15. Use neutral wording
16. Do not ask leading questions or questions that show bias.
17. Leave time for a General Question in the End
18. The last question should allow the interviewee to share any thoughts or opinions that they might want to share, such as "Thank you for all that valuable information, is there anything else you'd like to add before we end?"

1. Bring your questions to the interview
2. Explore the answers but return to your list of questions to follow your guide.
3. Record details such as the subjects name contact and details
4. Take detailed notes
5. Use empathy tools to encourage your participant to share information.
6. Final question: "Is there anything you think I should have asked that I didn't?"
7. Transcribe the interview
8. Write out both sides of the conversation, both question and answer.
9. Never change what the interviewee said or how they said it.
10. Outline the important points.
11. Edit the transcript for clarity, flow, and length.
12. Tell a story Now that you've gathered all of this great information and have accurately recorded it. It is important that you find a way to effectively document and share the story in a way that celebrates and accurately describes the story you were told.
13. Add details from your notes appearance and personality of your subject, ambient sounds, smells, visuals.
14. Check the facts.

Source: adapted from The Art of Interview" by Anne Williams

OBSERVATION

WHAT IS IT

This method involves observing people in their natural activities and usual context such as work environment. With direct observation the researcher is present and indirect observation the activities may be recorded by means such as video or digital voice recording.

WHY USE THIS METHOD

1. Allows the observer to view what users actually do in context.
2. Indirect observation uncovers activity that may have previously gone unnoticed

CHALLENGES

1. Observation does not explain the cause of behavior.
2. Obtrusive observation may cause participants to alter their behavior.
3. Analysis can be time consuming.
4. Observer bias can cause the researcher to look only where they think they will see useful information.

WHEN TO USE THIS METHOD

1. Know Context
2. Know User
3. Frame insights

HOW TO USE THIS METHOD

1. Define objectives
2. Define participants and obtain their cooperation.
3. Define The context of the observation: time and place.
4. In some countries the law requires that you obtain written consent to video people.
5. Define the method of observation and the method of recording information. Common methods are taking written notes, video or audio recording.
6. Run a test session.
7. Hypothesize an explanation for the phenomenon
8. Predict a logical consequence of the hypothesis
9. Test your hypothesis by observation
10. Analyze the data gathered and create a list of insights derived from the observations.

RESOURCES

Note pad
Pens
Camera
Video camera
Digital voice recorder

AFFINITY DIAGRAMS

WHAT IS IT?

Affinity diagrams are a tool for analyzing large amounts of data and discovering relationships which allow a design direction to be established based on the affinities. This method may uncover important hidden relationships.

Affinity diagrams are created through consensus of the design team on how the information should be grouped in logical ways.

WHO INVENTED IT?

Jiro Kawaita, Japan, 1960

WHY USE THIS METHOD?

Traditional design methods are less useful when dealing with complex or chaotic problems with large amounts of data. This method helps to establish relationships of affinities between pieces of information. From these relationships insights can be determined which are the starting point of design solutions. It is possible using this method to reach consensus faster than many other methods.

HOW TO USE THIS METHOD

1. Select your team
2. Place individual opinions or answers to interview questions or design concepts on post-it-notes or cards.
3. Spread post-it-notes or cards on a wall or large table.
4. Group similar items.
5. This can be done silently by your design team moving them around as they each see affinities. Work until your team has consensus.
6. Name each group with a different colored card or Post-it-note above the group.
7. Repeat by grouping groups.
8. Rank the most important groups.
9. Photograph results
10. Analyze affinities and create insights.
11. 5 to 20 participants

RESOURCES

White board
Large wall spaces or tables
Dry-erase markers
Sharpies
Post-it notes

HOW TO CREATE AN AFFINITY DIAGRAM

1 Collect more than 150 pieces of research data through ethnographic techniques such as interviews or observation. Put each piece of data on one card or post it note.

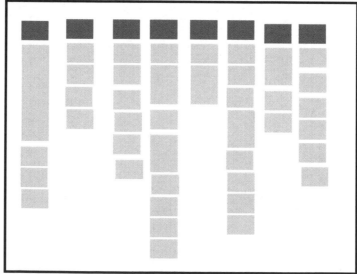

3 Ask your team without talking to arrange the post it notes into associated groups in vertical columns. Add a different colored header which describes what connects the data in each group.

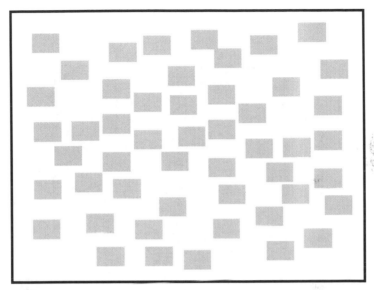

2 When you return to your office spread the post it notes or cards randomly on a large wall or table

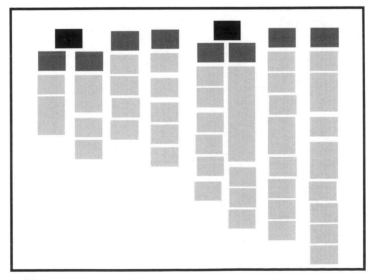

4 Crete super headers in a different color if groups can be combined. Organize groups into a hierarchy of importance of design issues to be addressed

FOCUS GROUPS

WHAT IS IT?
Focus groups are discussions usually with 6 to 12 participants led by a moderator. Focus groups are used during the design of products, services and experiences to get feedback from people

They are often conducted in the evening and take on average two hous. 8 to 12 questions are commonly explored in discussion.

WHO INVENTED IT?
Robert K. Merton 1940 Bureau of Applied Social Research.

WHY USE THIS METHOD?
1. Low cost per participant compared to other research methods.
2. Easier than some other methods to manage

CHALLENGES
1. Removes participants from their context
2. Requires a skilled moderator
3. Focus group study results may not be not be generalizable.
4. Focus group participants can influence each other.

HOW TO USE THIS METHOD
1. Select a good moderator.
2. Prepare a screening questionnaire.
3. Decide incentives for participants.
4. Select facility.
5. Recruit participants. Invite participants to your session well in advance and get firm commitments to attend. Remind participants the date of the event.
6. Participants should slt around a large table. Follow discussion guide.
7. Describe rules. Provide refreshments.
8. First question should encourage talking and participation.
9. The moderator manages responses and asks important questions
10. Moderator collects forms and debriefs focus group.
11. Analyze results while still fresh.
12. Summarize key points.
13. Run additional focus groups to deepen analysis.

RESOURCES
Sound and video recording equipment
White board
Post-it-notes

SYNTHESIS

"

Make sense from your research. What are the insights? What is connected? What are the unmet needs and desires of your audience? How can your design be unique, and better than what is already out there?

"

One of the symptoms
of an absence of
innovation is the fact
that you lose your
jobs

STEVE JOBS
Apple

SYNTHESIS

Synthesis is the convergent part of the design process.
Ideate: Explore and many possibilities as time and resources make possible. Select the most promising ideas. This can be done by a voting process with a group of stakeholders and your divers team. Implement: Build a series of prototypes to test. Evaluate: Test your prototypes with end users. Refine the prototype design and retest until you have something that works well.

ACTIONABLE INSIGHTS

Design Thinking provides insights that are based on unrecognized or unmet needs. An insight is a fresh point of view based on a deep understanding of the way of thinking and behavior. An insight occurs by mentally connecting two or more things that have not been connected before. These things may be things that many people have seen or experienced but not connected before. A goal of Design Thinking is to build actionable insights

USER NEED STATEMENT

The user need statement or question is the desires or needs of end users expressed in their own words.

User Need Statement
I am a doctor who has a hard time keeping babies warm.

POINT OF VIEW STATEMENT

A point-of-view (POV) is reframing of a design challenge into an actionable problem statement. The POV is used as the basis for design ideation. The POV defines the design intent.

The POV helps reframe the design problem into an actionable focus for the generation of ideas.

SERVICE BLUEPRINT TEMPLATE

	ACTIVITY PHASE	ACTIVITY PHASE	ACTIVITY PHASE	ACTIVITY PHASE	ACTIVITY PHASE	ACTIVITY PHASE
CUSTOMER ACTIONS	What does user do?					
TOUCHPOINTS	objects and places of customer contact					
LINE OF INTERACTION	what the customer finds unpleasant					
FRONT STAGE	What your Staff do					
LINE OF VISIBILITY						
BACK STAGE	What your Staff do					
OPPORTUNITIES	What your Staff do					

SERVICE BLUEPRINTS

WHAT IS IT?

A blueprint is a process map often used to describe the delivery of services information is presented as a number of parallel rows of activities. These are sometimes called swim lanes. They may document activities over time such as:

1. Customer Actions
2. Touch points
3. Direct contact visible to customers
4. Invisible back office actions
5. Support Processes
6. Physical Evidence
7. Emotional Experience for customer.

WHO INVENTED IT?

Lynn Shostack 1983

WHEN TO USE THIS METHOD

1. Know Context
2. Know User
3. Frame insights

WHY TO USE THIS METHOD

1. Can be used for design or improvement of existing services or experiences.
2. Is more tangible than intuition.
3. Makes the process of service development more efficient.
4. A common point of reference for stakeholders for planning and discussion.
5. Tool to assess the impact of change.

HOW TO USE THIS METHOD

1. Define the service or experience to focus on.
2. A blueprint can be created in a brainstorming session with stakeholders.
3. Define the customer demographic.
4. See though the customer's eyes.
5. Define the activities and phases of activity under each heading.
6. Link the contact or customer touchpoints to the needed support functions
7. Use post-it-notes on a white board for initial descriptions and rearrange as necessary drawing lines to show the links.
8. Create the blueprint then refine iteratively.

RESOURCES

Paper
Pens
White board
Dry-erase markers
Camera
Blueprint templates
Post-it-notes

EXPERIENCE MAP TEMPLATE

ANTICIPATE	ENTER	ENGAGE	EXIT	REVIEW

CUSTOMER ACTIVITIES	DOING	THINKING	FEELING	EMOTIONAL EXPERIENCE	OPPORTUNITIES

EXPERIENCE MAPS

WHAT IS IT?

It is a diagram that allows a designer to describe the elements of a customer experience in clear concise terms.

WHY USE THIS METHOD?

1. Helps develop a consistent, predictable customer experience.
2. Identifies problems in a customer experience and how to fix them.
3. Presents an overview of your customer's experience from their point of view.
4. Helps reduce the number of dissatisfied customers
5. A tool for developing more loyal customers
6. Can be used with different personas.
7. A focus for discussion between departments of an organization that helps develop a consistent and superior customer experience.
8. Can be used to understand where to place resources most efficiently

HOW TO USE THIS METHOD

1. Identify your team. Use a cross disciplinary team of 4 to 12 people with stakeholders.
2. Collect research data related to customer experience using ethnographic techniques such as interviews.
3. Identify the customer experience to be analyzed. Identify the context. Identify personas.
4. Break the customer experience down into sub activities and place each activity in a horizontal time-line
5. Below each activity describe what the customer is doing
6. Do one line of comments for what they are doing, one line for what they are thinking, and feeling.
7. Use post-it-notes to add positive and negative experiences to the relevant parts of the time line.
8. Brainstorm opportunities where customer experiences are negative.
9. When you are complete photograph the map and document it using a program such as Adobe Illustrator.
10. Circulate the map to stakeholders for feedback and refine.

PERSONA TEMPLATE

PERSONA NAME

DEMOGRAPHICS

Age
Occupation
Location

Income
Gender
Education

CHARACTERISTIC S

GOALS

What does this person want to achieve in life?

MOTIVATIONS

Incentives
Fear
Growth

Achievement
Power
Social

FRUSTRATIONS

What experiences does this person
wish to avoid?

QUOTE

Characteristic quote

BRANDS

What brands does this persona purchase or wish to purchase?

CHARACTERISTICS

EXTROVERT   **INTROVERT**

FREE TIME

TRAVEL

LUXURY GOODS

TECHNICAL SAVVY

SPORTS

SOCIAL NETWORKING

MOBILE APPS

PERSONAS

WHAT IS IT?

"A persona is a archetypal character that is meant to represent a group of users in a role who share common goals, attitudes and behaviors when interacting with a particular product or service Personas are user models that are presented as specific individual humans. They are not actual people, but are synthesized directly from observations of real people."(Cooper)

WHO INVENTED IT?

Alan Cooper 1998

WHY USE THIS METHOD?

1. Helps create empathy for users and reduces self reference.
2. Use as tool to analyze and gain insight into users.
3. Help in gaining buy-in from stakeholders.

HOW TO USE THIS METHOD

1. Inaccurate personas can lead to a false understandings of the end users. Personas need to be created using data from real users.
2. Collect data through observation, interviews, ethnography.
3. Segment the users or customers
4. Create the Personas
5. Avoid Stereotypes
6. Each persona should be different. Avoid fringe characteristics. Personas should each have three to four life goals which are personal aspirations,
7. Personas are given a name, and photograph.
8. Design personas can be followed by building customer journeys

RESOURCES

Raw data on users from interviews or other research Images of people similar to segmented customers.
Computer
Graphics software

PERCEPTUAL MAP

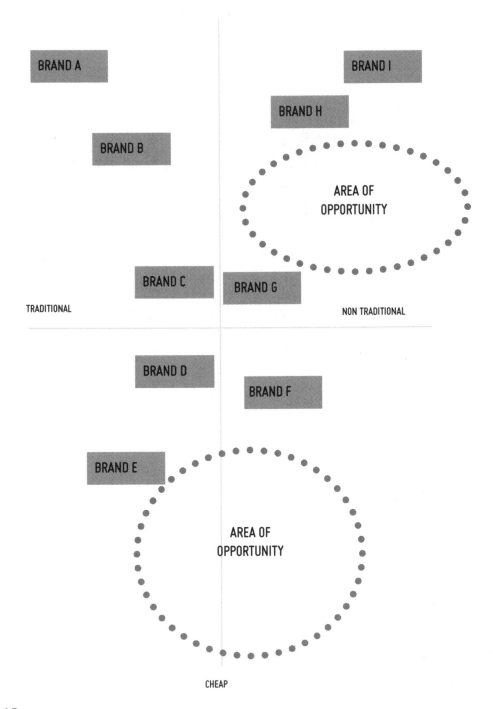

PERCEPTUAL MAPS

WHAT IS IT
Perceptual mapping is a method that creates a map of the perceptions of people of competing alternatives to be compared.

WHO INVENTED IT
Unknown

WHY USE THIS METHOD
1. Aids communication and discussion within the organization
2. To gain competitive advantage,
3. Helps build competitive strategy
4. Helps build communication strategy
5. Helps identify potential new products
6. Helps build brand strategy

CHALLENGES
1. Because the position of a product or service on the map is subjective, you can ask several people to locate the position through group discussion.
2. Works well for clearly defined functional attributes such as price, product features

WHEN TO USE THIS METHOD
1. Know Context
2. Know User
3. Frame insights
4. Explore Concepts

HOW TO USE THIS METHOD
1. Define characteristics of product or service to map.
2. Identify competing brands, services or products to map.
3. Map individual items.
4. Interpret the map.
5. Create strategy.

RESOURCES
1. Pen
2. Paper
3. White board
4. Dry erase markers

DESIGN THINKING MIND MAP

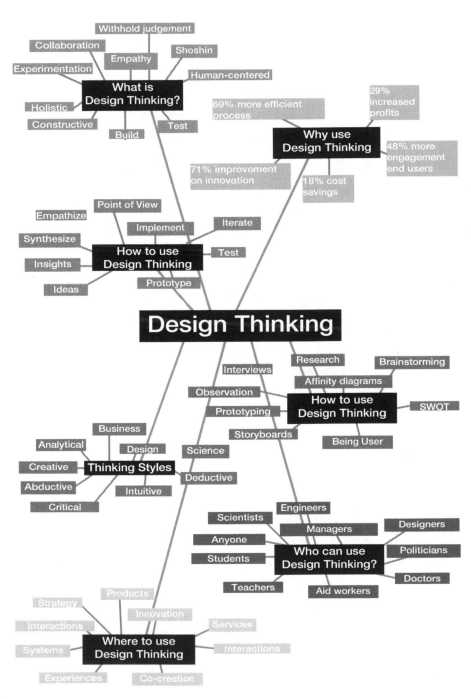

MIND MAPS

WHAT IS IT?

A mind map is a diagram used to represent the affinities or connections between a number of ideas or things. Understanding connections is the starting point for design. Mind maps are a method of analyzing information and relationships.

WHO INVENTED IT?

Porphry of Tyros 3rd century BC. Allan Collins, Northwestern University 1960, USA

WHY USE THIS METHOD?

1. The method helps identify relationships.
2. There is no right or wrong with mind maps. They help with they help with memory and organization.
3. Problem solving and brainstorming
4. Relationship discovery
5. Summarizing information
6. Memorizing information

CHALLENGES

Print words clearly, use color and images for visual impact.

HOW TO USE THIS METHOD

1. Start in the center with a key word or idea. Put box around this node.
2. Use images, symbols, or words for nodes.
3. Select key words.
4. Keep the key word names of nodes s simple and short as possible.
5. Associated nodes should be connected with lines to show affinities.
6. Make the lines the same length as the word/image they support.
7. Use emphasis such as thicker lines to show the strength of associations in your mind map.
8. Use radial arrangement of nodes.

RESOURCES

Paper
Pens
White board
Dry-erase markers

DESIGN BRIEF &
POINT OF VIEW

Define who your
audience is

Define the problem
that you will solve and
the need that you will
address

Define your unique
Point of View

SWOT ANALYSIS

WHAT IS IT?
SWOT Analysis is a useful technique for understanding your strengths and weaknesses, and for identifying both the opportunities open to you and the threats you face.

WHO INVENTED IT?
Albert Humphrey 1965 Stanford University

WHY USE THIS METHOD?
1. SWOT analysis can help you uncover opportunities that you can exploit.
2. You can analysis both your own organization, product or service as well as those of competitors.
3. Helps develop a strategy of differentiation.
4. It is inexpensive

CHALLENGES
1. Use only verifiable information.
2. Have system for implementation.

HOW TO USE THIS METHOD
1. Explain basic rules of brainstorming.
2. Ask questions related to the SWOT categories.
3. Record answers on a white board or video
4. Categorize ideas into groups
5. Consider when evaluating "What will the institution gain or lose?"

RESOURCES
Post-it-notes
SWOT template
Pens
White board
Video camera
Dry-erase markers

SWOT TEMPLATE

Strengths

Weaknesses

Opportunities

Threats

SAMPLE SWOT QUESTIONS

STRENGTHS

1. Advantages of proposition
2. Capabilities
3. Competitive advantages
4. Marketing - reach, distribution
5. Innovative aspects
6. Location and geographical
7. Price, value, quality?
8. Accreditation, certifications
9. Unique selling proposition
10. Human resources
11. Experience,
12. Assets
13. Return on investment
14. Processes, IT, communications
15. Cultural, attitudinal, behavioral
16. Management cover, succession

WEAKNESSES

1. Value of proposition
2. Things we cannot do.
3. Things we are not good at
4. Perceptions of brand
5. Financial
6. Own known vulnerabilities
7. Time scales, deadlines and pressures
8. Reliability of data, plan predictability
9. Morale, commitment, leadership
10. Accreditation,
11. Cash flow, start-up cash-drain
12. Continuity, supply chain robustness

OPPORTUNITIES

1. Market developments
2. Competitors' vulnerabilities
3. New USP's
4. Tactics - surprise, major contracts
5. Business and product development
6. Information and research
7. Partnerships, agencies, distribution
8. Industrial trends
9. Technologies
10. Innovations
11. Global changes
12. Market opportunities
13. Specialized market niches
14. New exports or imports
15. Volumes, production, economies
16. Seasonal, weather, fashion influences

THREATS

1. Political effects
2. Legislative effects
3. Obstacles faced
4. Insurmountable weaknesses
5. Environmental effects
6. IT developments
7. Competitor intentions
8. Loss of key staff
9. Sustainable financial backing
10. Market demand
11. New technologies, services, ideas

BACKCASTING

WHAT IS IT?

Backcasting is a method for planning the actions necessary to reach desired future goals. This method is often applied in a workshop format with stakeholders participating. The scenarios are developed for periods of between 1 and 20 years in the future.

The participants first identify their goals and then work backwards to identify the necessary actions to reach those goals.

WHO INVENTED IT?

AT&T 1950s, Shel 1970s

WHY USE THIS METHOD?

1. It is inexpensive and fast
2. Backcasting is a tool for identifying, planning and reaching future goals.
3. Backcasting provides a strategy to reach future goals.

CHALLENGES

1. Need a good moderator
2. Needs good preparation

RESOURCES

Post-it-notes
White board
Pens
Dry-erase markers

WHEN TO USE THIS METHOD

1. Define intent
2. Know Context
3. Know User
4. Frame insights
5. Explore Concepts
6. Make Plans
7. Deliver Offering

HOW TO USE THIS METHOD

A typical backcasting question is "How would you define success for yourself in 2015?

1. Define a framework
2. Analyze the present situation in relation to the framework
3. Prepare a vision and a number of desirable future scenarios.
4. Back-casting: Identify the steps to achieve this goal.
5. Further elaboration, detailing
6. Step by step strategies towards achieving the outcomes desired.
7. Ask do the strategies move us in the right direction? Are they flexible strategies?. Do the strategies represent a good return on investment?
8. Implementation, policy, organization embedding, follow-up

C-BOX

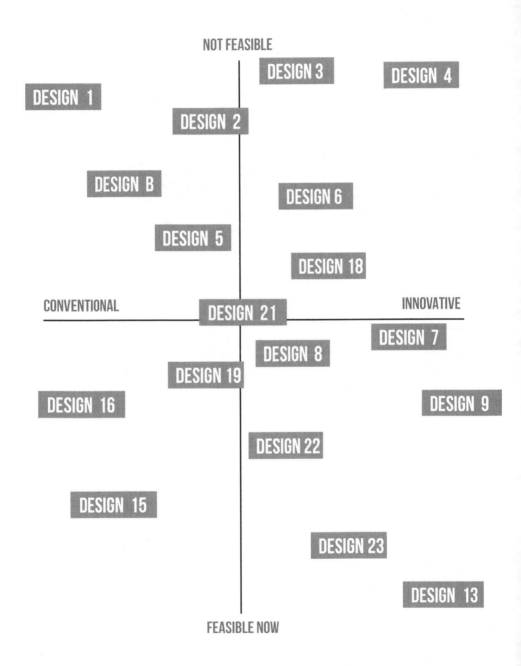

C-BOX

WHAT IS IT?

A C-box is a type of perceptual map that allows comparison and evaluation of a large number of ideas generated in a brainstorming session by a design team. The method allows everyone to contribute in a democratic way. It can be used to identify the most feasible and innovative ideas. It is up to your team to decide the level of innovation that they would like to carry forward from the idea generation or divergent phase of the project to the convergent or refinement and implementation phases.

WHO INVENTED IT?

Marc Tassoul, Delft 2009

WHY USE THIS METHOD?

1. It is democratic
2. It is quick and productive
3. It is inexpensive

WHEN TO USE THIS METHOD

1. Frame insights
2. Explore Concepts

HOW TO USE THIS METHOD

1. The moderator defines the design problem
2. You group can be optimally from 4 to 20 people.
3. On a white board or large sheet of paper create two axes. You can also use tape on a large wall.
4. Innovation on the horizontal and feasibility on the vertical axes creating 4 quadrants
5. The scale on the innovation ranges from not innovative at the left hand to highly innovative on the right hand end.
6. Alternative axes are attractiveness and functionality.
7. Brainstorm concepts. Each team member to generate 5 to 10 concepts over 30 minutes. One idea per post-it note. Hand out more post-it notes if required.
8. Each team member then presents each idea taking one to three minutes per idea depending on time available.
9. With the group's input discuss the ideas and precise position on the map.
10. Position each post-it-note according to the group consensus.

131

IDEATION

"

Use the diverse perspectives of the team members to create 75 to 120 good design solutions. that effectively balance the needs of people, appropriate use of technology and business goals. Keep an open mind until the ideas have been tested and compared

"

I have not failed. I've just found 10,000 ways that will not work

Just because something doesn't do what you planned it to do doesn't mean it's useless

To have a great idea have a lot of them

THOMAS EDISON
Design Thinker

BRAINSTORMING

PREPARING FOR BRAINSTORMING

Come to the brainstorm session prepared.

1. Bring a lot of paper and markers.
2. Pens
3. Post-it-notes
4. Index cards
5. A flip chart
6. White board or wall
7. Video camera
8. Camera
9. One clear goal per brainstorming session.
10. Determine who will write things down and document the proceedings?
11. Allow one to two hours for a brainstorming session.
12. Recruit good people.
13. 8 to 12 people is a good number
14. Prepare brainstorm questions that you think will help guide the group.

CREATE A STRATEGY

1. What do you want to achieve?
2. What problem do you want solved?
3. Define the goal
4. How will you define the problem to the participants?
5. How long will the session be?
6. How many people will be involved?
7. What will be the mix of people?
8. Will there be a follow up session?
9. Will you send out information before the session?
10. Do the participants have the information that they need?
11. Who should you invite?
12. Assemble a diverse team.
13. Do the participants have the right skills and knowledge for the task?
14. Where will the brainstorm be held?
15. Who owns the intellectual property?
16. Will the session be free of interruptions?
17. How will you record the ideas?
18. What will you do with the information?
19. What brainstorming technique will be used and is it best for your purpose?
20. Be mindful of the scope brainstorm questions. Neither too broad nor too narrow.
21. 45-60 minutes for brainstorm time. Warm up 15-30 minutes.
22. Wrap up 15-30 minutes.

CHOOSING A TECHNIQUE

1. There are many different brainstorming methods.
2. Choose a method that suites your task and participants
3. Try different methods over time to find which ones work best for you.

REFRESHMENTS

1. An army marches on it's stomach
2. Offer tea, coffee water, soda.

FACILITATING

1. Encourage everyone to contribute.
2. Review the rules and ask group to enforce them.
3. Encourage an attitude of shoshin.
4. Ask participants to turn phones off or onto vibrate mode.
5. A facilitator isn't a leader.
6. Do not steer the discussion
7. Do not let particular people dominate the conversation.
8. Keep the conversations on topic.
9. Set realistic time limits for each stage and be sure that you keep on time.
10. 5. Have a brainstorm plan and stick to it.
11. The facilitator should create an environment where it is safe to suggest wild ideas.
12. Provide clear directions at the beginning of the meeting.
13. Clearly define the problem to be discussed.
14. Write the problem on the white board where everyone can see it.
15. Provide next steps at the end of the meeting.
16. Select final ideas by voting.
17. Use your camera or phone to take digital pictures of the idea output at the end of your meeting.
18. Good facilitation requires good listening skills
19. The facilitator should run the white board, writing down ideas as people come up with them,
20. Prevent people from interrupting others
21. Invite quieter people to contribute.
22. Hire a facilitator if necessary.
23. Start on time.
24. End on time.
25. keep things moving
26. You can filter the best ideas after the session or get the team to vote on their preferred ideas during the session.
27. Listen
28. Write fast & be visual
29. Use humour and be playful
30. Thank the group after the session.
31. Provide next steps to the group after the meeting.
32. Keep participants engaged
33. Encourage inter activity
34. 100 ideas per hour.
35. Avoid social hierarchy
36. Organize small break-out sessions that cut across traditional office boundaries to establish teams.
37. Encourage passion.

Source Hasso Plattner Institute of Design Standford University

RULES FOR BRAINSTORMING

38. "Defer judgment Separating idea generation from idea selection strengthens both activities. For now, suspend critique. Know that you'll have plenty of time to evaluate the ideas after the brainstorm.
39. Encourage wild ideas
40. One conversation at a time Maintain momentum as a group. Save the side conversations for later.
41. Headline Capture the essence quickly "
42. Focus on quantity not on quality."

POST-IT VOTING

1. Give every participant 4 stickers and have everyone put stickers next to their favorite ideas.
2. Each person tags 3 favorite ideas
3. Cluster favorite ideas
4. Clustering of stickers indicate possible strong design directions.

GROUP REVIEW

Ask everyone to review the boards of ideas, and discuss the specific ideas or directions they like and why.

Source adapted from Hasso Plattner Institute of Design

THE ENVIRONMENT

5. Select a space not usually used by your team.

6. Refreshments
7. Find a comfortable quiet room
8. Comfortable chairs
9. No interruptions
10. Turn phones off
11. Go off-site. A new environment might spur creativity and innovation by providing new stimuli. Helps participants mentally distance themselves from ordinary perceptions and ways of thinking.
12. Location matters:
13. Use big visible materials for writing on
14. Keep the temperature comfortable Adequate lighting
15. Suitable external noise levels
16. A circular arrangement of seats allows participants to read body language and with no "head of the table."
17. Seats should be not too far apart
18. Have a space with a lot of vertical writing space.

METHODS OF ARRANGING IDEAS

1. 2X2 matrix
2. Clustering
3. Continuum
4. Concentric circles
5. Time-line
6. Pyramid
7. Prioritization
8. Adoption curve

635 BRAINSTORMING PROCESS

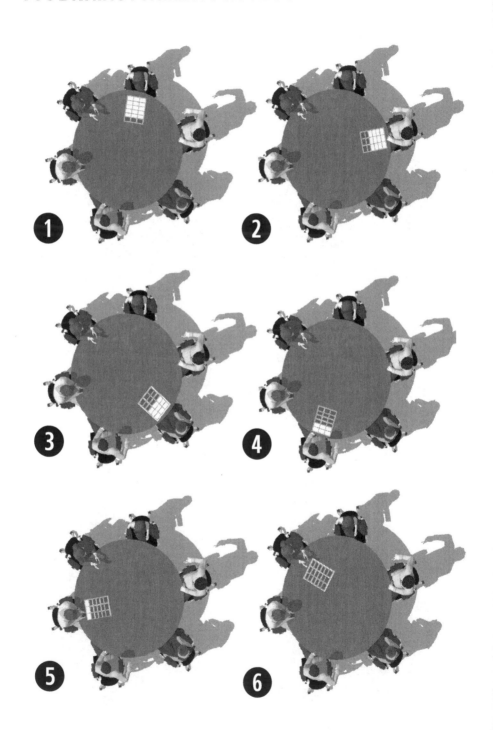

635 BRAINSTORMING

WHAT IS IT?
Method 635 is a structured form of brainstorming.

The outcome of each session is 108 ideas in 18 minutes.

WHO INVENTED IT?
Professor Bernd Rohrbach 1968

WHY USE THIS METHOD?
1. Can generate a lot of ideas quickly
2. Participants can build on each others ideas
3. Ideas are recorded by the participants
4. Democratic method.
5. Ideas are contributed privately.
6. Ideas are iteratively refined five times.
7. Does not need a moderator

WHEN TO USE THIS METHOD
1. Frame insights
2. Explore Concepts

HOW TO USE THIS METHOD
1. Your team should sit around a table.
2. Each team member is given a sheet of paper with the design objective written at the top.
3. The sheet can be divided into six rows of three boxes.
4. Each team member is given three minutes to generate three ideas.
5. Your participants then pass the sheet of paper to the person sitting on their left.
6. Each participant must come up with three new ideas.
7. The process can stop when sheets come around the table.
8. Repeat until ideas are exhausted. No discussion during the idea generating period.
9. Ideas can be sketches or written or a combination.
10. You can use an egg timer
11. You can also use post-it notes. One per box. This makes it easier to process the ideas after the session.
12. Analyze ideas as a group,
13. Put the ideas on a white board or wall cluster and vote for the preferred ideas.

RESOURCES
Large room
Large table
Paper
Pens
Post-it notes.

DRAW 10 ROWS OF TEN FAST SMALL SKETCHES

10 X 10 SKETCH METHOD

WHAT IS IT?

This method is an approach to making early concept generation sketching more efficient in use of time than the method that stresses finished sketches early in the design process. It allows more time to explore ideas and so stresses the quality of thinking and the final solution. The 10 x 10 method involves creating ten rows with ten thumbnail sketches per row on each page.

WHY USE THIS METHOD?

1. It allows more exploration of alternative ideas in a shorter time
2. May lead to a final concept which is a better design than traditional approaches.
3. Prevents sketches from becoming jewelry in the mind of the designer and more important than the quality of the final design solution.

CHALLENGES

1. This method takes discipline

HOW TO USE THIS METHOD

1. Traditional design concept exploration involves a designer producing six to 12 alternative design concepts presented as attractive renderings
2. This method involves a designer making ten rows of ten simple fast cartoon like sketches per page.
3. Each sketch should be no larger than one inch by one inch.
4. The designer produces 5 to 20 pages of very fast sketches during first phase of concept exploration
5. Designs are reviewed and ranked by the design team following a discussion and presentation by the designer and a relatively small number are selected for iteration, recombination and further development.
6. At the next stage more finished and larger concept sketches are produced

RESOURCES

Paper
Fine line pens
Sharpie markers

LOTUS TEMPLATE

A1	A2	A3	B1	B2	B3	C1	C2	C3
A4	**A**	A5	B4	**B**	B5	C4	**C**	C5
A6	A7	A8	B6	B7	B8	C6	C7	C8
D1	D2	D3	**A**	**B**	**C**	E1	E2	E3
D4	**D**	D5	**D**	■	**E**	E4	**E**	E5
D6	D7	D8	**F**	**G**	**H**	E6	E7	E8
F1	F2	F3	G1	G2	G3	H1	H2	H3
F4	**F**	F5	G4	**G**	G5	H4	**H**	H5
F6	F7	F8	G6	G7	G8	H6	H7	H8

LOTUS METHOD

WHAT IS IT?

The lotus blossom is a creativity technique that consists a framework for idea generation that starts by generating eight concept themes based on a central theme. Each concept then serves as the basis for eight further theme explorations or variations.

WHO INVENTED IT?

Yasuo Matsumura, Director of the Clover Management Research

WHY USE THIS METHOD?

1. This method requires that a quantity of 81 ideas is generated. To generate one good idea it is necessary to generate many ideas.
2. You can explore a spectrum of ideas from low risk to high risk or other spectrum.
3. Each idea can be developed in the outer boxes.

CHALLENGES

1. It is a somewhat rigid model. Not every problem will require the same number of concepts to be developed.

WHEN TO USE THIS METHOD

To generate concepts

HOW TO USE THIS METHOD

1. Draw up a lotus blossom template of 9 x 9 empty boxes.
2. Write the design problem in the center box of the diagram.
3. Write eight related ideas around the center.
4. Each idea then becomes the central idea of a new theme or blossom.
5. Follow step 3 with all central ideas.

RESOURCES

Paper
Pens
White board
or large sheet of paper
Dry-erase markers
Post-it-notes.

DOT VOTING

CONCEPT 1

● ● ● ● ● ●

CONCEPT 2

● ● ●

CONCEPT 3

● ● ● ●

CONCEPT 4

● ● ●

CONCEPT 5

●

CONCEPT 6

● ● ● ● ●

DOT VOTING

WHAT IS IT?
This is a way of efficiently selecting from a large number of ideas the preferred ideas to carry forward in the design process.

WHY USE THIS METHOD?
It is a method of selecting a favored idea by collective rather than individual judgment. It is a fast method that allows a design to progress. It leverages the strengths of diverse team member viewpoints and experiences.

CHALLENGES
1. The assessment is subjective.
2. Groupthink
3. Not enough good ideas
4. Inhibition
5. Lack of critical thinking

RESOURCES
Large wall
Adhesive dots

WHEN TO USE THIS METHOD
1. Define intent
2. Know Context
3. Know User
4. Frame insights
5. Explore Concepts
6. Make Plans
7. Deliver Offering

HOW TO USE THIS METHOD
1. Gather your team of 4 to 12 participants.
2. Brainstorm ideas for example ask each team member to generate ten ideas as sketches.
3. Each idea should be presented on one post-it-note or page.
4. Each designer should quickly explain each idea to the group before the group votes.
5. Spread the ideas over a wall or table.
6. Ask the team to vote on their two or three favorite ideas and total the votes. You can use sticky dots or colored pins to indicate a vote or a moderator can tally the scores.
7. Rearrange the ideas so that the ideas with the dots are ranked from most dots to least.
8. Refine the preferred ideas.

SCENARIOS

WHAT IS IT?

A scenario is a narrative or story about how people may experience a design in a particular future context of use. They can be used to predict or explore future interactions with concept products or services. Scenarios can be presented by media such as storyboards or video or be written. They can feature single or multiple actors participating in product or service interactions.

WHO INVENTED IT?

Herman Kahn, Rand Corporation 1950, USA

WHY USE THIS METHOD?

1. Scenarios become a focus for discussion which helps evaluate and refine concepts.
2. Usability issues can be explored at a very early stage in the design process.
3. The are useful tool to align a team vision.
4. Scenarios help us create an end to end experience.
5. Interactive experiences involve the dimension of time.
6. Personas give us a framework to evaluate possible solutions.

CHALLENGES

1. Generate scenarios for a range of situations.
2. Include problem situations
3. Hard to envision misuse scenarios.

WHEN TO USE THIS METHOD

1. Frame insights
2. Generate Concepts
3. Create Solutions

HOW TO USE THIS METHOD

1. Identify the question to investigate.
2. Decide time and scope for the scenario process.
3. Identify stakeholders and uncertainties.
4. Define the scenarios.
5. Create storyboards of users goals, activities, motivations and tasks.
6. Act out the scenarios.
7. The session can be videotaped.
8. Analyze the scenarios through discussion.
9. Summarize insights

RESOURCES

Storyboard templates
Pens
Video cameras
Props
White board
Dry-erase markers

SCAMPER

WHAT IS IT?
SCAMPER is a brainstorming technique and creativity method that uses seven words as prompts.
1. Substitute.
2. Combine.
3. Adapt.
4. Modify.
5. Put to another use.
6. Eliminate.
7. Reverse.

WHO INVENTED IT?
Alex Osborne

WHY USE THIS METHOD?
1. Scamper is a method that can help generate innovative solutions to a problem.
2. Leverages the diverse experiences of a team.
3. Makes group problem solving fun.
4. Helps get buy in from all team members for solution chosen.
5. Helps build team cohesion.
6. Everyone can participate.

CHALLENGES
1. Some ideas that you generate using the tool may be impractical.
2. Best used with other creativity methods

WHEN TO USE THIS METHOD
1. Generate concepts

HOW TO USE THIS METHOD
1. Select a product or service to apply the method.
2. Select a diverse design team of 4 to 12 people and a moderator.
3. Ask questions about the product you identified, using the SCAMPER mnemonic to guide you.
4. Create as many ideas as you can.
5. Analyze
6. Prioritize.
7. Select the best single or several ideas to further brainstorm.

RESOURCES
Pens
Post-it-notes
A flip chart
White board or wall
Refreshments

SCAMPER QUESTIONS

SUBSTITUTE

1. What materials or resources can you substitute or swap to improve the product?
2. What other product or process could you substitute?
3. What rules could you use?
4. Can you use this product in another situation?

COMBINE

1. Could you combine this product with another product?
2. Could you combine several goals?
3. Could you combine the use of the product with another use?
4. Could you join resources with someone else?

ADAPT

1. How could you adapt or readjust this product to serve another purpose or use?
2. What else is the product like?
3. What could you imitate to adapt this product?
4. What exists that is like the product?
5. Could the product adapt to another context?

MODIFY

1. How could you change the appearance of the product?
2. What could you change ?
3. What could you focus on to create more return on investment?
4. Could you change part of the product?

PUT TO ANOTHER USE

1. Can you use this product in another situation?
2. Who would find this product useful?
3. How would this product function in a new context?
4. Could you recycle parts of this product to create a new product?

ELIMINATE

1. How could you make the product simpler?
2. What features, parts, could you eliminate?
3. What could you understate or tone down?
4. Could you make the product smaller or more efficient?
5. What components could you substitute to change the order of this product?

DISNEY METHOD

WHAT IS IT?

The Disney Method is a parallel thinking technique. It was invented before Design Thinking evolved to it's current state but has many of the elements of the Design Thinking approach. It allows a team to discuss an issue from four perspectives. It involves parallel thinking to analyze a problem, generate ideas, evaluate ideas, and to create a strategy. It is a method used in workshops. The four thinking perspectives are Spectators, Dreamers, Realists and Critics.

WHO INVENTED IT?

Dilts, 1991

WHY USE THIS METHOD?

1. Allows the group to discuss a problem from four different perspectives

CHALLENGES

1. An alternative to De Bono Six Hat Method.
2. Can deliver a workable solution quickly.

WHEN TO USE THIS METHOD

1. Explore Concepts

HOW TO USE THIS METHOD

1. Have Four different brainstorming sessions in four different rooms.
2. At the end of each of the four sessions the participants leave the room and then at a later time reenter the next room then assuming the personas and perspectives of the next group. Time taken is often 60 to 90 minutes per session. The sessions adopt the following themes.
3. The spectator's view. Puts the problem in an external context. How would a consultant, a customer or an outside observer view the problem?
4. The Dreamers view. Looking for an ideal solution. What would our dream solution for this be? What if? Unconstrained brainstorm.
5. Realists view. The realists are convergent thinkers. How can we turn the dreamer's views into reality? Looking for ideas that are feasible, profitable, customer focused and can be implemented within 18 months.
6. The Critics view. What are the risks and obstacles? Who would oppose this plan? What could go wrong? Refine, improve or reject. Be constructive.

DESIGN CHARRETTES

WHAT IS IT?

A design Charrette is a collaborative design workshop usually held over one day or several days. Charrettes are a fast way of generating ideas while involving diverse stakeholders in your decision process. Charrettes have many different structures and often involve multiple sessions. The group divides into smaller groups. The smaller groups present to the larger group.

WHO INVENTED IT?

The French word, "charrette" spelt with two r's means "cart" This use of the term is said to originate from the École des Beaux Arts in Paris during the 19th century, where a cart, collected final drawings while students finished their work.

WHY USE THIS METHOD?

1. Fast and inexpensive.
2. Increased probability of implementation.
3. Stakeholders can share information.
4. Promotes trust.

CHALLENGES

1. Managing workflow can be challenging.
2. Stakeholders may have conflicting visions.

RESOURCES

Large space
Tables
Chairs
White boards
Dry erase markers
Camera
Post-it notes

PROTOTYPE

"

Make your ideas
tangible with a series
of fast, inexpensive
prototypes.

Ask people to give you
feedback and use it to
improve the designs.

> Learning and innovation go hand in hand. The arrogance of success is to think that what you did yesterday will be sufficient for tomorrow

WILLIAM POLLARD
Physicist

LOW FIDELITY PROTOTYPING

WHAT IS IT?

Low Fi prototyping is a quick and cheap way of gaining insight and informing decision-making without the need for costly investment. Simulates function but not aesthetics of proposed design. Prototypes help compare alternatives and help answer questions about interactions or experiences.

WHY USE THIS METHOD?

1. May provide the proof of concept
2. It is physical and visible
3. Inexpensive and fast.
4. Useful for refining functional and perceptual interactions.
5. Assists to identify any problems with the design.
6. Helps to reduce the risks
7. Helps members of team to be in alignment on an idea.
8. Helps make abstract ideas concrete.
9. Feedback can be gained from the user

CHALLENGES

1. A beautiful prototype completed too early can stand in the way of finding the best design solution.

WHEN TO USE THIS METHOD

1. Know Context
2. Know User
3. Frame insights
4. Explore Concepts

HOW TO USE THIS METHOD

1. Construct models, not illustrations
2. Select the important tasks, interactions or experiences to be prototyped.
3. Build to understand problems.
4. If it is beautiful you have invested too much.
5. Make it simple
6. Assemble a kit of inexpensive materials
7. Preparing for a test
8. Select users
9. Conduct test
10. Record notes on the 8x5 cards.
11. Evaluate the results
12. Iterate

RESOURCES

Paper
Cardboard
Wire
Foam board,
Post-it-notes
Hot melt glue

LOW FIDELITY PROTOTYPE KIT

Here are some suggestions for a kit of materials to help you construct low fidelity prototypes

1. Copy paper
2. Magnets
3. Snaps
4. Masking tape
5. Duct tape (color would be ideal)
6. Tape
7. Post-it notes
8. Glue sticks
9. Paper clips, (asst colors ideal)
10. Decorative brads (square, crystal)
11. Hole punch
12. Scissors
13. Stapler (with staples)
14. Hot glue
15. Glue guns
16. Rulers
17. Pipe Cleaners
18. Colored card
19. Zip ties
20. Foam core sheets
21. Velcro
22. Rubber bands, multicolored
23. Assorted foam shapes
24. Markers
25. Scissors
26. Glue sticks
27. Tape
28. Glue guns
29. Straws
30. Paper Clips
31. Construction Paper
32. ABS sheets
33. Felt
34. Foam sheets
35. String
36. Foil
37. Butcher paper
38. Stickers
39. Pipe cleaners
40. Popsicle sticks
41. Multicolored card

DARK HORSE PROTOTYPE

WHAT IS IT?

A dark horse prototype is your most creative idea built as a fast prototype. The innovative approach serves as a focus for finding the optimum real solution to the design problem.

WHO INVENTED IT?

One of the methods taught at Stanford University.

WHY USE THIS METHOD?

1. This method is a way of breaking free of average solutions and exploring unknown territory
2. A way of challenging assumptions.

CHALLENGES

1. Fear of unexplored directions
2. Fear of change
1. Designers can become too attached to their prototypes and allow them to become jewelry that stands in the way of further refinement.
2. Client may believe that system is real.

WHEN TO USE THIS METHOD

1. Explore Concepts

HOW TO USE THIS METHOD

1. After initial brainstorming sessions select with your team the most challenging, interestingly or thought provoking idea.
2. Build also a prototype of your idea that best balances business, human needs with appropriate use of technology
3. Create a low resolution prototype of the two selected ideas
4. Test with end users
5. With your team analyze and discuss the prototype.
6. Brainstorm ways of bringing back the dark horse concept into a realizable solution.
7. Refine and implement.

STORYBOARD TEMPLATE

PROJECT	NAME	DATE	PAGE

DIALOGUE

ACTION

PROJECT	NAME	DATE	PAGE

DIALOGUE

ACTION

PROJECT	NAME	DATE	PAGE

DIALOGUE

ACTION

STORYBOARDS

WHAT IS IT?

The storyboard is a narrative tool derived from cinema. A storyboard is a form of prototyping which communicates each step of an activity, experience or interaction. Used in films and multimedia as well as product and UX design. Storyboards consists of a number of 'frames' that communicate a sequence of events in context.

WHO INVENTED IT?

Invented by Walt Disney in 1927. Disney credited animator Webb Smith with creating the first storyboard. By 1937-38 all studios were using storyboards.

WHY USE THIS METHOD?

1. Can help gain insightful user feedback.
2. Conveys an experience.
3. Can use a storyboard to communicate a complex task as a series of steps.
4. Allows the proposed activities to be discussed and refined.
5. Storyboards can be used to help designers identify opportunities or use problems.

HOW TO USE THIS METHOD

1. Decide what story you want to describe.
2. Choose a story and a message: what do you want the storyboard to express?
3. Create your characters
4. Think about the whole story first rather than one panel at a time.
5. Create the drafts and refine them through an iterative process. Refine.
6. Illustrations can be sketches or photographs.
7. Consider: Visual elements, level of detail, text, experiences and emotions, number of frames, and flow of time.
8. Keep text short and informative.
9. 6 to 12 frames.
10. Tell your story efficiently and effectively.
11. Brainstorm your ideas.

RESOURCES

Pens
Digital camera
·Storyboard templates
Comic books for inspiration

VIDEO PROTOTYPING

WHAT IS IT?

Video prototypes use video to illustrate how users will interact with a new system. Video prototypes can be thought of as sketches that illustrate what the interaction with the new system will be like.

WHY USE THIS METHOD?

1. Capturing an experience over time requires a linear medium like video

2. Video prototypes are a good way of communicating a complex system of interactions in an easy to access way that can be shared with a large number of people.

HOW TO USE THIS METHOD

1. Choose a director and a camera person.

2. Decide who the kactors are and who will create the storyboard and props.

3. Decide how you will communicate the story: title-cards only, an off-camera voice-over or through dialog.

4. Storyboard the sequence of shots.

5. Begin by shooting the initial title card 4 seconds with the name of the project, group, date, time and version number.

6. Shoot a title card 6 seconds that identifies the personas and the context.

7. Shoot an establishing shot that shows the user(s) in context.

8. Shoot the series of interaction points that tell the story and communicate the interaction.

9. Use mid shots to show conversation and close-ups to show devices.

10. "Editing-in-the-camera" involves shooting each sequence of the video prototype in the order that it will be viewed, so that it does not need to be edited afterwards.

11. Some video prototypes use a narrator or voice over, others use only title cards others rely on the actors to explain interactions.

RESOURCES

Video camera
Smart phone camera
Card for titles
Simple props
Actors
Lights
Post-it-notes

WIREFRAMING

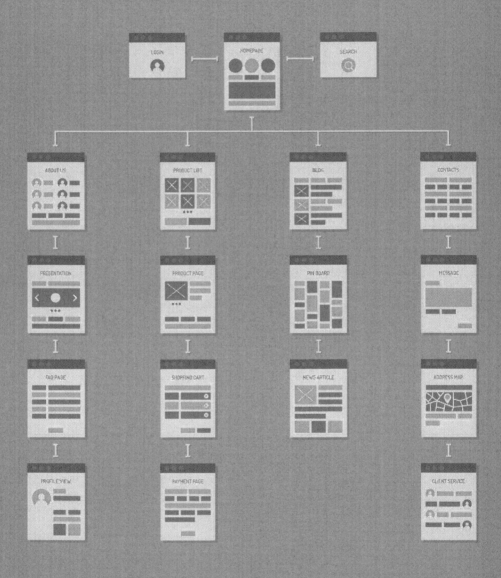

WIREFRAMING

WHAT IS IT?

Website wireframes are a simplified outline of the elements of a web page. They are useful for communicating the functionality of a website in order to get feedback on the design. The wireframe depicts the page layout, interface and navigation, and how these elements interact in use.

WHO INVENTED IT?

Matthew Van Horn claims to have invented the term around 1994 in New York.

WHY USE THIS METHOD?

1. Wireframes are useful for getting feedback on a design.
2. Wireframes can speed up the iteration process of a website design.
3. Enable on-line collaboration
4. Helps Identify needed changes early on in the development.
5. Wireframes are low cost

CHALLENGES

1. Notes to explain behavior are useful
2. Wireframes do not explain interactive details involving movement.

WHEN TO USE THIS METHOD

1. Define intent
2. Know Context
3. Know User
4. Frame insights
5. Explore Concepts

HOW TO USE THIS METHOD

1. There are a several ways to create wireframes. These include drawing by hand. Using Adobe Photoshop or Illustrator and using wireframe software.
2. Start by listing all of the elements that you want on your website.
3. Use simple boxes or outlines of the shape of elements, and name them. These elements can include: navigation: buttons, Company logo: can just be represented by a box, content areas and search box.
4. Review your design and adjust as necessary.
5. Make wireframe for each page in your site.

RESOURCES

Paper
Pens
Wireframe software
Computer

ROLE PLAYING

WHAT IS IT

Role playing is a research method where the researcher physically acts out the interaction or experience of the user of a product, service or experience. It is a type of prototyping, a narrative or story about how people may experience a design in a particular future context. Role playing can be used to predict or explore future interactions with concept products or services.

WHY USE THIS METHOD

1. Role playing helps a designer gain empathy and insights into the experience of the user.
2. Useful for unfamiliar situations.
3. It is a physical activity so may uncover insights not apparent when using storyboarding
4. It helps designers empathize with the intended users and their context.
5. Is an inexpensive method requiring few resources.

CHALLENGES

1. It is difficult to envision all the ways a product or service could be misused.
2. Some people feel self conscious when asked to role play

RESOURCES

Note pad
Pens
Video camera
Empathy tools

HOW TO USE THIS METHOD

1. Identify the situation.
2. Identify scenarios and tasks users undertake.
3. Create storyboards.
4. Assign roles.
5. Isolate moments where the users interact with the product or service.
6. Use your own intuitive responses to iterate and refine the design.
7. This method can be used to test physical prototypes.
8. You can act out the tasks in the environments or context of use.
9. You can use empathy tools such as glasses to simulate the effects of age or a wheelchair.
10. Consider typical misuse cases.
11. Discuss insights.

ITERATE

Modify the design prototype and test and refine until it works

"

"You never learn by doing something right 'cause you already know how to do it. You only learn from making mistakes and correcting them."

RUSSELL AKOFF
Professor Emeritus of Management Science
at the Wharton School, University of Pennsylvania

"

An architect's most useful tools are an eraser at the drafting board and a wrecking ball at the site

FRANK LLOYD WRIGHT
Architect

DO A REALITY CHECK

At each milestone in a design development, the design team and important stakeholders such as customers, clients, manufacturers representatives can meet and review the design to see how real the solution is and refine the direction as necessary.

IDENTIFY STAKEHOLDERS FOR FEEDBACK

OBTAIN FEEDBACK

Usability testing is a technique used in user-centered interaction design to evaluate a product by testing it on users. Usability testing focuses on measuring a designs fitness for an intended purpose. Usability testing involves observation under controlled conditions to determine how well people can use the design

1. Methods include:
2. Hallway testing five to six people are brought in to test the product, or service. The name of the technique refers to the fact that the testers should be random people who pass by in the hallway.
3. Remote usability Usability evaluators, developers and end users are located in different countries and time zones, .
4. Expert review. Involves bringing in experts with experience in the field to evaluate the usability of a product system or service.

5. Automated expert review Automated expert reviews provide usability testing but through the use of programs given rules for good design and heuristics. Though an automated review might not provide as much detail and insight as reviews from people, they can be finished more quickly and consistently.
6. A/B Testing. Two versions (A and B) are compared, which are identical except for one variation that might impact a user's behaviour.

TEST

Create a series of fast prototypes to test your design direction

"

A designer is anyone
who plots change for the
better.

MARTIN NEULLER
Design Thinker

OBTAIN FEEDBACK

Usability testing is a technique used in user-centered interaction design to evaluate a product by testing it on users. Usability testing focuses on measuring a designs fitness for an intended purpose. Usability testing involves observation under controlled conditions to determine how well people can use the design

1. Methods include:
2. Hallway testing five to six people are brought in to test the product, or service. The name of the technique refers to the fact that the testers should be random people who pass by in the hallway.
3. Remote usability Usability evaluators, developers and end users are located in different countries and time zones, .
4. Expert review. Involves bringing in experts with experience in the field to evaluate the usability of a product system or service.
5. Automated expert review Automated expert reviews provide usability testing but through the use of programs given rules for good design and heuristics. Though an automated review might not provide as much detail and insight as reviews from people, they can be finished more quickly and consistently.
6. A/B Testing. Two versions (A and B) are compared, which are identical except for one variation that might impact a user's behaviour.

DESIGN REVIEW QUESTIONS

1. Does the design conform to the design intent statement?
2. Is the design achievable?
3. Have the important risks been identified?
4. Is the design a solution to an identified need or problem?
5. What is the business case?
6. Is the design consistent?
7. Is the design as simple as possible?
8. Are the components recyclable?
9. Can the design be scaled?
10. Are all features necessary?
11. Is everything documented?
12. What are the risks associated with this design?
13. Are any new risks posed by the design that have not been identified?
14. Are the interfaces identified
15. Is the design consistent with the context?
16. Have critical features and interactions been prototyped and tested?
17. Is the cost of ownership reduced?
18. Is the design easy to maintain?
19. Have all legal requirements and regulations been addressed?

20. Have the key stakeholders been identified and involved?
21. What were the assumptions?
22. Is the design usable and accessible?
23. How will the design be implemented?
24. What is the scope of the design?
25. What design alternatives were considered?

TEST

The product, service or experience is tested, Improvements are made. The process is not over until the design works. The prototype may not work as well as expected, New ideas may need to be brainstormed and the prototype modified and retested

REFINE AND TEST AGAIN

Review you video of end users interacting with your prototype. Get feedback from as many stakeholders as possible including end users, and your design team. Brainstorm a list of insights generated. Brainstorm how the design could be improved to overcome any issues that you have seen. Refine your prototype build in the feedback and test it again. Go though this iterative process as many times as is necessary till your design works well for your intent.

HEURISTIC EVALUATION

Heuristic evaluation is an evaluation of by one or more experts. The experts measure the usability, efficiency, and effectiveness of the interface based on 10 usability heuristics defined by Jakob Nielsen in 1994.

Nielsen's Usability Heuristics, which have continued to evolve in response to user research and new devices, include:

1. Visibility of System Status
2. Match Between System and the Real World
3. User Control and Freedom
4. Consistency and Standards
5. Error Prevention
6. Recognition Rather Than Recall
7. Flexibility and Efficiency of Use
8. Aesthetic and Minimalist Design
9. Help Users Recognize, Diagnose, and Recover from Errors
10. Help and Documentation

MAKE A VIDEO

Record the end user interacting with existing products and services as well as your prototypes. Recording the activity in it's natural setting will help you understand the subtle and complex nature of an activity and can be used for feedback from stakeholders to refine the design direction.

The first known ethnographic film was made by in 1895 by Felix-Louis Regnault who filmed a Senegalese woman making pots

Joseph Schaeffer suggested that there are at least four ways that video can be useful .
1. Videos allow for coverage of complex activities in their natural settings over an extended period of time.
2. Videos can increase quality and reliability of observations made regarding the activity.
3. Videos can be reviewed by researchers and participants which can help increase the scope and quality of understanding the activity.
4. Videos can be used to establish connections between understandings and the observed activities.

The sooner and more often you invite feedback, the better that your final design will be.
You do not discover the problems until you show your design to the stakeholders and ask for their feedback. Note the problems each time you get feedback and fix them. This is the process that Thomas Edison used to invent the first usable light bulb and that James Dyson used to invent the world's most successful vacuum cleaner. You can apply this iterative process to any type of design.

"

Few ideas work
on the first try.
Iteration is key to
innovation

SEBASTIAN THRUN
Director of the Artificial Intelligence
Laboratory at Stanford University.

IMPLEMENT & DELIVER

Manufacture your
design. Distribute it
and sell it.

TEST AND EVALUATE

Testing is one of the core activities of Design Thinking The design team checks design capabilities, requirements by testing with end users and the ability to meet these, and epitomizing the design to combine these two. Testing is carried out with consumers through observation, focus groups and other methods. Testing and learning through feedback are activities in each design phase.

FINALIZE YOUR PRODUCTION DESIGN

The details of this phase will depend on the type of design area that you are working in.

BUILD EXTERNAL PARTNERSHIPS

Collaboration with other organizations and individuals is becoming an integral part of the design process. Organizations benefit from their partners' insights and expertise. Many of the best ideas have emerged not through the inspiration of a single mind, but through the exchange of ideas.

SIGN OFF FROM STAKEHOLDERS

When you believe that you have a design that can be distributed and sold, show it to all your stakeholders one last time before documenting the design for final manufacture.

MAKE YOUR PRODUCTION SAMPLES

AUTHORIZE VENDORS

Manufacture first samples Review first production with vendors.

LAUNCH

At this point in the design process the product or service is launched, and the process now includes liaison with appropriate internal teams in areas such as marketing, communications, packaging and brand.

1. How can you make it impossible for this to fail?
2. Decide on your goals.
3. Prepare.
4. Make it fun and interesting
5. Set a date.

PRE-LAUNCH

1. 3-4 weeks of pre-launch
2. Create the campaign.
3. Evoke emotion.
4. Create desire.
5. Prepare marketing materials.
6. Do something original.
7. Review what's working.
8. Create urgency.

MID-LAUNCH

1. Publish your blog post, send out your email announcement.
2. Post on social media and other various communication channels.
3. Listen and respond.

POST-LAUNCH

1. Have a party!
2. Ask for feedback from first buyers
3. Deliver a bonus that wasn't expected
4. Make it memorable.
5. Review and improve.

6. Plan ahead.

Source: Adapted from Jonathan Mead
"The 40 Step Checklist for a Highly Successful Launch"

DELIVER
Do final testing obtain sign off from stakeholders and launch. The design should successfully address the problem identified in the user research phase of the process.

Key activities and objectives during the Deliver stage are:

1. Final testing, approval and launch
2. Targets, evaluation and feedback loops.

DID THE DESIGN MEET IT'S GOALS?
Ideas that have emerged during the design process or in post-launch feedback may be put to one side but developed later, and will then go through the design process again on its own.

MEASURE SUCCESS
1. Determine how you will measure the success
2. 2 to 3 months after release measure the success
3. Measure the success and objectively evaluate.
4. Implement metrics and measurements

SOME WAYS TO MEASURE SUCCESS:
1. Customer satisfaction

2. ROI is standard business measure of project profitability, over the market life of the design expressed as a percentage of initial investment.
3. Increased usage
4. Increased revenue from existing customers
5. The ability of your product to solve the problem
6. New customer acquisition
7. Product margin
8. Cash flow
9. Product Team's satisfaction
10. Improved customer retention rate
11. Increased market share

WHAT COULD BE IMPROVED?
Invite customers to co-create, and integrate feedback.

DEFINE NEXT VISION
The design process is never complete. Now it is time to start planning the next product or service so that you can stay ahead of the many competitors.

Source: Adapted from Jonathan Mead
"The 40 Step Checklist for a Highly Successful Launch"

EXERCISES

"

Design Thinking is
a human-centered
approach to
innovation that draws
from the designer's
toolkit to integrate
the needs of people,
the possibilities of
technology, and the
requirements for
business success

TIM BROWN
CEO IDEO

DESIGN THINKING RESOURCES

1. Good size collaborative space
2. Large table
3. Chairs
4. Adhesive dots
5. Copy Paper
6. Markers and pens
7. Cutting mat
8. Scissors
9. Glue
10. Masking tape
11. Push pins
12. Printer
13. Projector
14. Video camera
15. Post-it-notes
16. Foam core boards
17. Cardboard
18. White-board
19. Large wall
20. Large Pin board
21. Prototyping kit

LOW FIDELITY PROTOTYPE KIT

1. Copy paper
2. Magnets
3. Snaps
4. Masking tape
5. Duct tape (color would be ideal)
6. Tape
7. Post-it notes
8. Glue sticks
9. Paper clips, (asst colors ideal)
10. Decorative brads (square, crystal)
11. Hole punch
12. Scissors
13. Stapler (with staples)
14. Hot glue
15. Glue guns
16. Rulers
17. Pipe Cleaners
18. Colored card
19. Zip ties
20. Foam core sheets
21. Velcro
22. Rubber bands, multicolored
23. Assorted foam shapes
24. Markers
25. Scissors
26. Glue sticks
27. Tape
28. Glue guns
29. Straws
30. Paper Clips
31. Construction Paper
32. ABS sheets
33. Felt
34. Foam sheets
35. String
36. Foil
37. Butcher paper
38. Stickers
39. Pipe cleaners
40. Popsicle sticks
41. Multicolored card

WARMING UP

Instructions
Break your team into groups of two people.
Each person should partner with someone they do not know if possible. Warming up exercises help stimulate constructive interaction, help people get to know each other and contribute effectively. Do one of the following exercises:

Who am I?
Duration: 3 minutes
Draw or write a one sentence description of something that represents yourself.
Duration 2 minutes per person
Each person introduces themselves to the group using their sketch or description.

Common ground
Duration: 5 minutes
Each person should interview their partner and make a list of 3 things that they have in common.

Desert Island
Duration: 3 minutes
Each person should list 3 things that they would take if that was all they could take to a desert island.
Duration 2 minutes per person
Introduce yourself to the group using your list.

Outcomes
Duration: 5 minutes
Each person should sketch or write what they believe could be the best possible outcome for the project.
Duration 2 minutes per person
Each person introduces themselves to the group using their sketch or description.

Resources
Copy paper
Markers
White board

INTERVIEW

Instructions

Divide your team into groups of two. Each team member should interview their partner for 15 minutes to identify an unmet product or service need that they have. It should be something that can be actionable to design with available time and resources and that others also need.

Who is the audience?
Age, gender, geography culture

What is it?
Describe the unmet need

Why is it needed?

Where would it be used?

When would it be used?

How would it be used?

IDENTIFY KEY STAKEHOLDERS

Key stakeholders

Identify the stakeholders who may be affected by your design. They can be people or organizations. Stakeholders are those who can have a positive or negative effect the success of your design. They can be recruited to give you useful feedback.

End-users

1.
2.
3.
4.

Vendors

1.
2.
3.
4.

Community

1.
2.
3.
4.

Organizations

1.
2.
3.
4.

Employees

1.
2.
3.
4.

RESEARCH QUESTIONS

Instructions

Identify five people who may be prospective customers or end users related to the possible product or service that you identified in the previous stage. Interview each of the five people and when you are finished answer the following questions. Be prepared to change your targets based on what you discover.

Who are the competitors?

Name five products or services that compete in your target area.

What are the problems with the competitive designs?

Name one significant problem with each competitive design

What are the top 3 problems with the competitive designs?

List the 3 top problems in a hierarchy of importance

Ask why there is a need five times?
1.
2.
3.
4.
5.
Dig deeper until you understand the underlying need

What is the most significant underlying need for the design?

What insights did you discover?

SYNTHESIS QUESTIONS

Instructions
Explore the following questions in an interview with each participant.

Customer Segments
Identify three groups of customers who need this design

Value Proposition
What is the unique value proposition for each of 3 segments

Activities
What activities are needed to support the value propositions?
Name 3 activities

Channels
What channels could the design be distributed through? For example on-line or stores. Name 3 channels.

Revenue
What are customers willing to pay for? For example monthly fee or retail price. Name 3 revenue streams.

Resources
What resources would be needed to implement your business?
For example on-line storage. name three resources needed.

Partners
What partners would be needed to implement your business?
Name 3 partners.

Costs
Name your businesses 3 main costs?

Source: Adapted from Alexander Oswalder Business Model Canvas

YOUR ANSWERS

Customer Segments
1.
2.
3.

Value Proposition
1.
2.
3.

Activities
1.
2.
3.

Channels
1.
2.
3.

Revenue
1.
2.
3.

Resources
1.
2.
3.

Partners
1.
2.
3.

Main Costs
1.
2.
3.

SWOT TEMPLATE

Strengths

Weaknesses

Opportunities

Threats

POINT OF VIEW QUESTIONS

Instructions

What are your goals?
Answer the following questions

Specific

What will you design?

Measurable

How will you know when you have the best solution.
How will you measure progress toward your goal?

Attainable

Is your goal a possible to achieve with your time and resources?

Realistic

Is your goal realistic and within your reach? Are you willing to commit to your goal?

Relevant

Is your goal relevant to your long term needs?

Time

What is your target time-frame to reach the gaols?

IDEATION INSTRUCTIONS

Instructions

Generate 12 simple cartoon sketches that may be good design solutions for your user need.

Answer in one sentence each of the following questions for each design

For each design solution answer the following questions:

1. What unmet user needs does the design address?
2. How does the design utilize technology processes and materials to best advantage?
3. Why is the design a good business solution?
4. Who are the target audience for each design?
5. How is this design a better design than existing competitive designs?

PROTOTYPE

Create a low fidelity prototype of your favored design

Here are some suggestions for a kit of materials to help you construct low fidelity prototypes

Copy paper
Magnets
Snaps
Masking tape
Duct tape (color would be ideal)
Tape
Post-it notes
Glue sticks
Paper clips, (asst colors ideal)
Decorative brads (square, crystal)
Hole punch
Scissors
Stapler (with staples)
Hot glue
Glue guns
Pipe Cleaners
Colored card
Zip ties
Rubber bands, multicolored
Assorted foam shapes
Markers
Paper Clips
Construction Paper
ABS sheets
Felt
Foam sheets
String
Foil
Butcher paper
Popsicle sticks

TEST QUESTIONS

Instructions

Use some of the materials on the facing page to make a fast prototype of your design. Show the prototype to five people and ask them to answer the following questions.

What works in the design?

1.

2.

3.

4.

What doesn't work in the design?

1.

2.

3.

4.

What refinements need to be made?

1.

2.

3.

4.

ITERATION QUESTIONS

Instructions

Modify and improve your prototype based on your previous feedback. Show it to five people and answer the following questions.

What works in the design?

1.

2.

3

4.

What doesn't work in the design?

1.

2.

3.

4.

What refinements need to be made?

1.

2.

3.

4.

TEMPLATES

"

We interrogate the world by making"

PERSONA TEMPLATE

PERSONA NAME

DEMOGRAPHICS

Age	Income
Occupation	Gender
Location	Education

CHARACTERISTIC S

GOALS

What does this person want to achieve in life?

MOTIVATIONS

Growth	Achievement
Incentives	Power
Fear	Social

FRUSTRATIONS

What experiences does this person wish to avoid?

QUOTE

Characteristic quote

BRANDS

What brands does this persona purchase or wish to purchase?

CHARACTERISTICS

EXTROVERT   **INTROVERT**

TRAVEL

TECHNICAL SAVVY

SOCIAL NETWORKING

FREE TIME

LUXURY GOODS

SPORTS

MOBILE APPS

STORYBOARD TEMPLATE

PROJECT   NAME   DATE   PAGE

DIALOGUE   DIALOGUE   DIALOGUE

ACTION   ACTION   ACTION

PROJECT   NAME   DATE   PAGE

DIALOGUE   DIALOGUE   DIALOGUE

ACTION   ACTION   ACTION

PROJECT   NAME   DATE   PAGE

DIALOGUE   DIALOGUE   DIALOGUE

ACTION   ACTION   ACTION

635 BRAINSTORM TEMPLATE

PROBLEM STATEMENT:

	IDEA 1	IDEA 2	IDEA 3
1			
2			
3			
4			
5			
6			

CONTEXT MAP

	TRENDS	UNCERTAINTIES	TECHNOLOGY	USER NEEDS	ECONOMIC	POLITICAL	TRENDS

COMPETITOR MATRIX

BRAND	BRAND A	BRAND B	BRAND C	BRAND D
BRAND STATEMENT				
VALUE PROPOSITION				
TARGET CUSTOMERS				
BUSINESS MODEL				
TECHNOLOGY				
ENVIRONMENTAL PERFORMANCE				
KEY DIFFERENTIATION				

EVALUATION MATRIX

CRITERIA	WEIGHT	DESIGN A		DESIGN B		DESIGN C		DESIGN D	
		SCORE	WEIGHTED	SCORE	WEIGHTED	SCORE	WEIGHTED	SCORE	WEIGHTED
TOTAL									

PERCEPTUAL MAP TEMPLATE

SPIDER DIAGRAM TEMPLATE

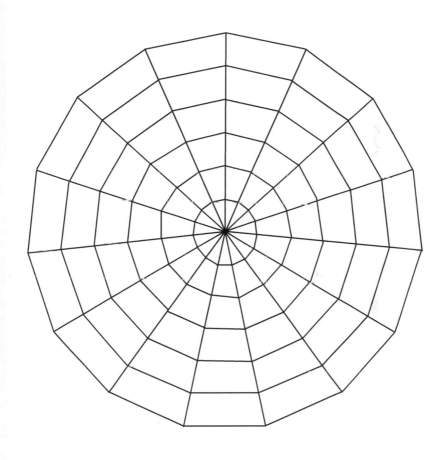

STAKEHOLDER POWER INFLUENCE MAP

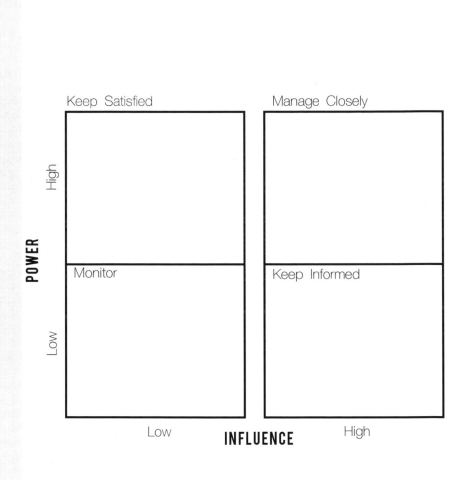

Keep Satisfied Manage Closely

Monitor Keep Informed

POWER

High

Low

INFLUENCE

Low High

DESIGN THINKING RUBRIC

LEVEL	EXCEEDS EXPECTATIONS	STRONG	EFFECTIVE	DEVELOPING	EMERGING	NEEDS IMPROVEMENT
SCORE	6	5	4	3	2	1
AMBIGUITY	Comfortable when things are unclear	Comfortable when things are unclear	Limited comfort when things are unclear	Limited comfort when things are unclear	Uncomfortable when things are unclear	Uncomfortable when things are unclear
EMPATHY AND HUMAN VALUES	Sees and understands others point of view. Focuses on user needs	Sees and understands others point of view. Focuses on user needs	Has limited understanding of other points of view	Has limited understanding of other points of view	Sees only own point of view	Sees only own point of view
COLLABORATIVE	Collaborates effectively with people from other disciplines with different backgrounds and viewpoints	Collaborates effectively with people from other disciplines with different backgrounds and viewpoints	Collaborates with people from other disciplines with different backgrounds and viewpoints in a limited way	Collaborates with people from other disciplines with different backgrounds and viewpoints in a limited way	Cannot collaborate with other. Sees only own point of view.	Cannot collaborate with other. Sees only own point of view.
CURIOUS	Is interested in things that are not understood and seeing things with fresh eyes.	Is interested in things that are not understood and seeing things with fresh eyes.	Shows limited interest in things that are not understood and seeing things with fresh eyes.	Shows limited interest in things that are not understood and seeing things with fresh eyes.	Is not interested in things that are not understood and seeing things with fresh eyes.	Is not interested in things that are not understood and seeing things with fresh eyes.
HOLISTIC	Balances perspectives of business, human values, the environment and technology	Balances perspectives of business, human values, the environment and technology	Considers the perspectives of business, human values, the environment and technology in a limited way	Considers the perspectives of business, human values, the environment and technology in a limited way	Does not consider the bigger context focusses on only one aspect such as business profitability	Does not consider the bigger context focusses on only one aspect such as business profitability
NON JUDGMENTAL	Crafts ideas with no judgement of the idea or idea creator	Crafts ideas with no judgement of the idea or idea creator	Some judgement of ideas and other idea creators	Some judgement of ideas and other idea creators	Extensive judgement of ideas and other idea creators	Extensive judgement of ideas and other idea creators
OPEN MINDSET	Is able to tackle problems regardless of industry or scope. Out of the box thinker	Is able to tackle problems regardless of industry or scope. Out of the box thinker	Can address problems over a number of industries and a limited range of scope	Can address problems over a number of industries and a limited range of scope	Can only address problems in a single industry of limited scope	Can only address problems in a single industry of limited scope
BIAS TOWARD ACTION	Creates prototypes and physical embodiments of ideas and actions that effectively move project forward	Creates prototypes and physical embodiments of ideas and actions that effectively move project forward	Creates some prototypes and progress but in a limited way	Creates some prototypes and progress but in a limited way	Talks about ideas but does not create physical prototypes or move project forward through actions	Talks about ideas but does not create physical prototypes or move project forward through actions
EXPERIMENTAL	Embraces experiment as an integral part of work	Embraces experiment as an integral part of work	Experiments in a limited way	Experiments in a limited way	Does not experiment	Does not experiment
COMPLEXITY	Creates clarity from complexity	Creates clarity from complexity	Limited ability to address complex problems	Limited ability to address complex problems	Cannot address complex problems	Cannot address complex problems
PROCESS	Is mindful of process	Is mindful of process	Follows process in a limited way	Follows process in a limited way	Has no process	Has no process
SHOSHIN	An attitude of openness, eagerness, and lack of preconceptions even when at an advanced level,	An attitude of openness, eagerness, and lack of preconceptions even when at an advanced level,	Some openness, and eagerness. Some preconceptions	Some openness, and eagerness. Some preconceptions	Lack of openness, and eagerness. Many preconceptions	Lack of openness, and eagerness. Many preconceptions
ITERATIVE	Makes improvements with prototyping feedback loops and cycles regardless of design phase	Makes improvements with prototyping feedback loops and cycles regardless of design phase	Limited ability to refine or improve ideas through iterative user feedback and prototyping	Limited ability to refine or improve ideas through iterative user feedback and prototyping	No ability to refine or improve ideas through iterative user feedback and prototyping	No ability to refine or improve ideas through iterative user feedback and prototyping

DO AN ON-LINE PROGRAM

If you liked this book and want to learn more about Design Thinking we regularly offer on-line classes and courses presented by the author. They are held at different times of day to suit your schedule and time zone.

You can find more information and register at the URL below and order print copies of this book or on Amazon soon.

Half day introductory workshop
http://dccintrodesignthinking.
eventbrite.com

Five week and 8 week on-line
certificate programs
http://dcc-designthinking.
eventbrite.com

Design Thinking process and
Methods Manual
400 pages
https://www.createspace.
com/4127650

We have presented many face to
face in-house workshops in global
locations. If you would like more
information related to creating a
custom workshop for your team
contact us at
info@curedale.com

OTHER TITLES IN THE SERIES

DESIGN THINKING
PROCESS AND METHODS MANUAL
Author: Robert A Curedale
Published by:
Design Community College Inc.
Edition 1 January 2013
398 pages
ISBN-10:   0988236214
ISBN-13:   978-0-9882362-1-9

DESIGN THINKING POCKET GUIDE
EDITION 1
Author: Curedale, Robert A
Published by:
Design Community College, Inc
Jun 01 2013
198 pages
ISBN-10: 098924685X
ISBN-13: 9780989246859

50 BRAINSTORMING METHODS
FOR TEAM AND INDIVIDUAL IDEATION
Author: Robert A Curedale
Published by:
Design Community College Inc.
Edition 1 January 2013
184 pages
ISBN-10:   0988236230
ISBN-13:   978-0-9882362-3-3

CHINA DESIGN INDEX 2014
China Design Index 2014
Author: Curedale, Robert A
Published by:
Design Community
College, Inc.
Edition 1 Feb 01 2014
384 pages
ISBN-10:1940805090
ISBN-13: 9781940805092

INTERVIEWS OBSERVATION AND FOCUS
GROUPS
Author: Curedale, Robert A
Published by:
Design Community College, Inc.
Edition 1 Apr 01 2013
188 pages
ISBN-10:0989246833
ISBN-13: 9780989246835

MAPPING METHODS
Author: Curedale, Robert A
Published by:
Design Community College, Inc.
Edition 1 Apr 01 2013
136 pages
ISBN-10: 0989246825
ISBN-13: 9780989246828

SERVICE DESIGN
Author: Curedale, Robert A
Published by:
Design Community College, Inc.
Edition 1 Aug 01 2013
372 pages
ISBN-10:0989246868
ISBN-13: 9780989246866

SERVICE DESIGN POCKET GUIDE
Author: Curedale, Robert A
Published by:
Design Community College, Inc.
Edition 1 Sept 01 2013
206 pages
ISBN-10:0989246884
ISBN-13: 9780989246880

DESIGN RESEARCH METHODS
150 WAYS TO INFORM DESIGN
Author: Curedale, Robert A
Published by:
Design Community College, Inc.
Edition 1 January 2013
290 pages
ISBN-10: 0988236257
ISBN-13: 978-0-988-2362-5-7

50 SELECTED DESIGN METHODS
Author: Curedale, Robert A
Published by:
Design Community College, Inc.
Edition 1 Jan 17 2013
114 pages
ISBN-10:0988236265
ISBN-13: 9780988236264

DESIGN METHODS 1
200 WAYS TO APPLY DESIGN THINKING
Author: Robert A Curedale
Published by:
Design Community College Inc.
Edition 1 November 2013
396 pages
ISBN-10:0988236206
ISBN-13:978-0-9882362-0-2

DESIGN METHODS 2
200 MORE WAYS TO APPLY DESIGN THINKING
Author: Robert A Curedale
Published by:
Design Community College Inc.
Edition 1 January 2013
398 pages
ISBN-13: 978-0988236240
ISBN-10: 0988236249

30 GOOD WAYS TO INNOVATE
Author: Curedale, Robert A
Published by:
Design Community College, Inc.
Edition 1 November 2015
108 pages
ISBN-10: 1940805139
ISBN-13: 978-1940805139

DCC ONLINE DESIGN EDUCATION

Start today, DCC expert online programs for designers and managers. More accessible than traditional design education and better value. Classes for different world time zones. Connect to classes anywhere with an internet connection. Study from home or train your whole team in your office. Free textbook with most courses. Check links below for all scheduled dates and local time calculator. Contact us at info@curedale.com for current information.

30 GOOD WAYS TO INNOVATE
https://dcc-30waystoinnovate.eventbrite.com

DESIGNING WITH COLOR
http://dcc-designingwithcolor.eventbrite.com

INTRODUCTION TO DESIGN THINKING
http://dccintrodesignthinking.eventbrite.com

DESIGN THINKING ONLINE PROGRAMS
http://dcc-designthinking.eventbrite.com

CREATING EXPERIENCE MAPS, JOURNEY MAPS, AND SERVICE BLUEPRINTS
http://dcc-experiencemaps.eventbrite.com

INTRO TO SERVICE DESIGN
http://dcc-introservicedesign.eventbrite.com

SERVICE DESIGN ONLINE PROGRAMS
http://dcc-servicedesign.eventbrite.com

INTRODUCTION TO DESIGN RESEARCH
http://dcc-introdesignresearch.eventbrite.com

DESIGN RESEARCH ONLINE PROGRAMS
http://dcc-designresearch.eventbrite.com

INTRODUCTION TO INDUSTRIAL DESIGN
http://www.eventbrite.com/e/introduction-to-industrial-design-tickets-16591880762

INDUSTRIAL DESIGN ONLINE PROGRAMS
http://dcc--industrialdesign.eventbrite.com

DESIGN RESEARCH: INTERVIEWING & FOCUS GROUPS
https://dcc-interviewsandfocusgroups.eventbrite.com

CREATING A SUCCESSFUL DESIGN PORTFOLIO
http://dcc-portfolio.eventbrite.com

PRODUCT DESIGN PROPOSALS
https://dcc-designproposals.eventbrite.com

INTRODUCTION TO HUMAN FACTORS ONLINE
http://dcc-humanfactors.eventbrite.com

DESIGN SYNTHESIS
http://dcc-designsynthesis.eventbrite.com

DESIGN IDEATION METHODS
https://dcc-ideation.eventbrite.com

INDEX

INDEX

V

W

ABOUT THE AUTHOR

Rob Curedale was born in Australia and worked as a designer, director and educator in leading design offices in London, Sydney, Switzerland, Portugal, Los Angeles, Silicon Valley, Detroit, and Hong Kong. He designed or managed the design of over 1,000 products as a consultant and in-house design leader for the world's most respected brands. Rob has three decades experience in every aspect of product development and design research, leading design teams to achieve transformational improvements in operating and financial results. Rob's design s can be found in millions of homes and workplaces around the world and have generated billions of dollars in corporate revenues.

Design practice experience
HP, Philips, GEC, Nokia, Sun, Apple, Canon, Motorola, Nissan, Audi VW, Disney, RTKL, Governments of the UAE,UK, Australia, Steelcase, Hon, Castelli, Hamilton Medical, Zyliss, Belkin, Gensler, Haworth, Honeywell, NEC, Hoover, Packard Bell, Dell, Black & Decker, Coleman and Harmon Kardon. Categories including furniture, healthcare, consumer electronics, sporting, housewares, military, exhibits, and packaging.

Teaching experience
Rob has taught as a full time professor, adjunct professor and visiting instructor at institutions including the following: Art Center Pasadena, Art Center Europe, Yale School of Architecture, Pepperdine University, Loyola University, Cranbrook Academy of Art, Pratt, Otis, a faculty member at SCA and UTS Sydney, Chair of Product Design and Furniture Design at the College for Creative Studies in Detroit, then the largest product design school in North America, Cal State San Jose, Escola De Artes e Design in Oporto Portugal, Instituto De Artes Visuals, Design e Marketing, Lisbon, Southern Yangtze University, Jiao Tong University in Shanghai and Nanjing Arts Institute in China.

Awards
Products that Rob has designed and managed the design of have been recognized with IDSA IDEA Awards, Good Design Awards UK, Australian Design Awards, and a number of best of show innovation Awards at CES Consumer Electronics Show. His designs are in the Permanent collections of a number of museums including the Powerhouse Design Museum. In 2013 Rob was nominated for the Advanced Australia Award. The Awards celebrate Australians living internationally who exhibit "remarkable talent, exceptional vision, and ambition." In 2015 Rob was selected with a group of leading international industrial designers to provide opening comments for the international congress of societies of industrial design conference ICSID in Gwangju, South Korea.

"

Around here, we do not look backwards for very long. We keep moving forward, opening up new doors and doing new things, because we're curious and curiosity keeps leading us down new paths."

WALT DISNEY
American entrepreneur, cartoonist, animator, voice actor, film producer and Design Thinker